62
Nonalcoholic
Dirty Sodas,
Punches & More
to Celebrate!

PARTY DRINKS

REBECCA HUBBELL

FOUNDER OF *SUGAR AND SOUL*

ROCK
POINT

First published in 2023 by Rock Point,
an imprint of The Quarto Group,
142 West 36th Street, 4th Floor,
New York, NY 10018, USA
T (212) 779-4972 F (212) 779-6058
www.Quarto.com

Rock Point titles are also available at discount for
retail, wholesale, promotional, and bulk purchase.
For details, contact the Special Sales Manager by
email at specialsales@quarto.com or by mail at The
Quarto Group, Attn: Special Sales Manager, 100
Cummings Center Suite 265D, Beverly, MA 01915 USA.

10 9 8 7 6 5 4 3 2 1

ISBN: 978-1-63106-951-2

Library of Congress Cataloging-in-Publication Data

Names: Hubbell, Rebecca, author.
Title: Party drinks : 62 nonalcoholic dirty sodas,
punches & more to celebrate / by Rebecca Hubbell.
Description: New York, NY, USA : Rock
  Point, an imprint of The Quarto Group,
  2023. | Includes index. | Summary: "Party
  Drinks includes 62 delicious recipes for sweet,
  flavorful, alcohol-free beverages great for
  family gatherings, special occasions, parties,
  and individual enjoyment."-- Provided by
  publisher.
Identifiers: LCCN 2023005015 (print) | LCCN
  2023005016 (ebook) | ISBN 9781631069512 |
  ISBN 9780760383049 (ebook)
Subjects: LCSH: Non-alcoholic cocktails.
Classification: LCC TX815 .H84 2023 (print)
  | LCC TX815 (ebook) | DDC 641.87/5--dc23
  eng/20230207
LC record available at https://lccn.loc
  gov/2023005015
LC ebook record available at https://lccn.loc
  gov/2023005016

Publisher: Rage Kindelsperger
Editorial Director: Erin Canning
Creative Director: Laura Drew
Managing Editor: Cara Donaldson
Editor: Keyla Pizarro-Hernández
Cover Design: Marisa Kwek
Interior Design: Tara Long

Printed in China

To Matthew

Master of fauxjitos and time management.

To Evangeline, Natalie, and Sereia

Masters of spills and making me late for everything.

You're my favorite people to share bubbles with.
Cheers to us and this crazy life together!

CONTENTS

Introduction 7
Drink Success 11
Tips & Tricks 15
Tools You'll Need 19

DIRTY SODAS

The OG Dirty Soda 24
Dirty Shirley 27
Mango Lassi 28
Breakfast Soda 31
Strawberries & Cream 32
Dirty Mule 35
Strawberry Colada 36
Orange Dream 39
Italian Cream Soda 40
Rocket Pop 43
Caramel Apple Lollipop 44
Twilight Swim 47
Southern Delight 48
Bohemian Raspberry 51
Boardwalk Sunset 52
Butterbeer 55
Cauldron Bubbles 56
Black Forest 59
American Pie 60
Santa Baby 63

SPRITZERS & REFRESHERS

Raspberry Lime Rickey 66
Coffee Soda 69
Island Breeze 70
Mom Juice 73
Blueberry Lavender Spritzer 74
Fauxjito 77
Mango Berry Splash 78
Balsamic Fizz 81
Blackberry Bramble 82
Winter Spritzer 85

FLOATS & MILKSHAKES

Root Beer Float 88
Lemonade Float 91
Brown Cow Float 92
Pineapple Orange Float 95
Shirley Temple Float 96
Chocolate Milk Float 99
Coconut Lime Sherbet Float 100
Purple Cow Float 103
Cookies 'n' Coffee Milkshake 104
Birthday Cake Milkshake 107
Malted Chocolate Milkshake 108
PB & J Milkshake 111

LEMONADES & ICED TEAS

Roasted Lemonade 114

Sparkling Berry Lemonade 117

Sparkling Mint Lemonade 118

Lavender Lemonade 121

Maple Lemonade 122

Island Palmer 125

Raspberry Iced Tea 126

Sparkling Blueberry Iced Tea 129

Peach Iced Tea 130

Strawberry Sweet Tea 133

PARTY PUNCHES

Love Potion Punch 136

Leprechaun Punch 139

Easter Bunny Punch 140

Brunch Punch 143

Sparkling Summer Punch 144

Baby Shower Punch 147

Trick-or-Treat Punch 148

Thanksgiving Punch 151

Jingle Bells Punch 152

Midnight Kiss Punch 155

HOMEMADE COMPONENTS

Classic Simple Syrup 158

Grenadine Simple Syrup 158

Brown Sugar Cinnamon Simple Syrup 159

Fruit Simple Syrup 160

Mint Simple Syrup 161

Flavored Simple Syrup 162

Lavender Simple Syrup 163

Chocolate Simple Syrup 164

Cold Brew Coffee 165

Unsweetened Iced Tea 166

Roasted Lemon Juice 167

Pudding Whipped Cream 168

Whipped Cream 169

Coffee Ice Cubes 170

Ice Ring & Ice Cups 171

Index 172
Acknowledgments 174
About the Author 176

INTRODUCTION

SPECIAL DRINKS FOR ANY OCCASION

As a '90s kid, my formative years were basically fueled by Mtn Dew® Code Red, Slush Puppies, and Kool-Aid. We'd ride our bikes two miles to the store just to get one—it wasn't about the soda really, it was about the adventure. As we got older and learned to drive, grabbing a drink at the store was no longer the thrilling escapade it once was. But there's still hope...

For me, drinks are an exciting way to break the ice and add a creative element to any event. Planning a fun menu is next-level hospitality and your friends and family will love that the drinks were more than an afterthought. And that's part of why drinks are such a big part of my food blog, *Sugar and Soul.*

It's important to me that my readers have the tools they need to create a memorable meal or throw a fantastic party with great food from start to finish, and drinks are an essential part of that. Over the last decade, millions of people have used my drink recipes to make the everyday special and the special days epic!

Fun, sugary, and nonalcoholic drinks can still play a big part in all of life's moments, big and small—birthdays, game nights, picnics, it doesn't matter.

When people host or attend a party and someone asks what to bring, the answer is usually "bring whatever you want to drink," and that, my friends, is a missed opportunity. Don't worry, I used to be that person too, but a decade of mixing drinks has taught me that what you serve matters. Think about it: What's the first thing you offer a guest? It's almost always a drink, so set the tone with something new and totally different, like a dirty soda.

Soda at its core is syrup and soda water, but what makes it dirty is adding extra flavors and cream so it becomes over the top and fun. I guarantee that you've had one of these drinks in some form or another, even if you're still not sure what they are.

Around the time most of us started turning to lighter drink options, such as seltzer and flavored water, Utah-based companies sort of secretly kickstarted the dirty soda craze by serving up custom sugary drinks with lots of carbonation and an optional splash of cream. Recently, the trend has broken out of the Mountain West, and now everyone wants to try the sweet and fizzy drinks that social media is slurping up every last drop of.

Chances are the sober curious movement and the rise in mocktail popularity is here to stay, and with it comes fresh ideas like dirty sodas and refreshers. My hope is that this collection of intentionally fun and nonalcoholic drinks makes you feel like you don't need to miss out on the ritual of having a cocktail, because you can still have a crafted beverage in hand that's creative and delicious.

Recipes like the Fauxjito (page 77) and Dirty Mule (page 35) are perfect for those who love the classics, and the Breakfast Soda (page 31) and Sparkling Mint Lemonade (page 118) are wonderful options for those looking to try something a little more contemporary.

Personally, I don't normally go for the typical soda flavors; my favorite is cream soda, which you'll find in my homemade Butterbeer (page 55), and in the summertime, nothing quite beats a bottle of ice-cold blueberry soda. And few things excite me more than discovering a bottle of Jones Fufu Berry at a convenience store!

My oldest child is all about "special drinks" right now. She primarily drinks water and seltzer, aka "bubbles," but from time to time it's fun to play in the kitchen and let her build her own mix of soda, juices, and simple syrup. She'll even ask me to photograph it for her "just like mommy does," so we have to make sure it's garnished too.

I love making these drinks with her and watching her discover new flavors and combinations. My counters usually end up super sticky, but it's worth it for the memories. And these are the memories I want to help you build with the recipes and knowledge I'm handing over to you in this book.

I hope this book inspires you to think beyond the food you're serving and start creating and incorporating specialty drinks that everyone will be talking about. All the drinks here can be styled as cool and easy additions to pretty much any occasion. The next time you have company, you'll be telling them to just bring themselves, because you've got the drinks covered!

Cheers,

REBECCA

DRINK SUCCESS

MORE THAN ANYTHING, I want to make sure that this book sets you up for success. In this section we'll discuss the variety of ingredients I recommend having on hand to make these delicious drink recipes. Most are easy to locate and purchase at your local supermarket or online, and some are even easy enough to make yourself right at home.

SODAS

This book features a variety of sodas in many flavors. In most of these recipes you can use your favorite brand. There are a lot of instances where a recipe calls for orange or lemon-lime soda, but in others you will find that the recipe calls for a specific brand and flavor, such as Jones Berry Lemonade, but I have made sure that all of the sodas used in this book are widely available in-store or online.

Here are some of the soda flavors you'll want to have on hand when making these recipes:

* Lemon-lime
* Root beer
* Strawberry
* Orange
* Cream soda
* Dr Pepper
* Coke or other cola
* Jones Berry Lemonade
* Jones Green Apple
* Club soda
* Grape soda

You'll also need a selection of flavored seltzer water if you plan to make any of the refresher recipes. I recommend my preferred brands throughout the book, but feel free to use your favorites.

SIMPLE SYRUPS

It's really easy to make simple syrup right at home. For most recipes, you'll want to use a 1:1 ratio of water and sugar to make a traditional simple syrup with granulated sugar or even a brown sugar version. Recipes like Grenadine Simple Syrup (page 158) and Chocolate Simple Syrup (page 164), while technically simple syrups, are prepared a little differently.

If you choose to purchase simple syrups instead of preparing them at home, that is completely fine. I recommend the Torani brand, but the Monin brand is also a great choice—they have a wide range of flavors and are available online for a reasonable price and fast shipping. I use many Torani brand syrups for a lot of recipes in this book when I don't want to make any of the syrups at home, and I love that they have a longer shelf life than homemade ones. However, you can use any brands of your choice or that are available to you, just note that there might be slight flavor variations between different brands and compared to the homemade recipes, too.

FRUITS & HERBS

Many fruits and herbs lend themselves nicely to making homemade simple syrups, but some provide better overall results than others. Berries, stone fruits, and fresh herbs like rosemary and mint respond nicely to the process and yield delicious results.

CREAM

A key ingredient used in the dirty soda recipes in this book is cream. You'll want to make sure to use a quality full-fat variety of cream for the best results, such as heavy cream or whipping cream. However, a light cream or even half-and-half can be used if preferred. I prefer cream by Hood, Shamrock Farms, or Horizon. For a nondairy option, I would recommend using Silk's Dairy Free Heavy Whipping Cream Alternative.

LEMONADE, ICED TEA & COFFEE

I have included recipes for each of these within the book, but if you find yourself short on time or are looking for a simpler option, you can purchase them instead. For lemonade, I prefer Newman's Own brand, because it has a lovely balance of sweet and tart and is the closest to the Roasted Lemonade (page 114) in terms of flavor. For iced tea, I usually prefer Pure Leaf unsweetened tea, but Gold Peak has a nice flavor too. For the cold brew coffee, I recommend using Chobani brand; it has a smooth but strong flavor that isn't overpowered by mixing with other ingredients. La Colombe and Chameleon are also great options but are more expensive.

CHOCOLATE

Dutch-processed or unsweetened cocoa powder will be necessary in the Chocolate Simple Syrup recipe (page 164) that's used to make several drinks in this book.

ICE

In the dirty soda recipes, nugget or crushed ice tends to work the best in floating the cream. This is mainly for looks since the dirty sodas are best enjoyed mixed, but I felt like it was an important thing to note. Nugget ice will dilute the dirty soda drinks quicker than traditional ice cubes, but this is okay since these drinks are on the sweeter side. If you don't feel like splurging on a machine, most of the fast-food restaurants that use nugget ice also sell it by the bag! For any drinks made without cream, or if you don't care whether the drink mixes when preparing, you can use traditional ice cubes unless otherwise stated in the recipe. You're also going to love the Coffee ice-cube trick (page 170) and the pretty ice cups and ice ring (page 171) that I use for punches too.

SALT & SPICES

A handful of the drinks in this book will require salt and spices. The salt is just to add a bit of gusto to some of the milkshakes —table or sea salt will work great. For the spices, some of the drinks, like the Mango Lassi (page 28) calls for a dash of cardamom. The Thanksgiving Punch (page 151) will require some whole spices, such as cinnamon sticks, whole cloves, and allspice berries.

GARNISHES & TOPPINGS

Don't underestimate the power of a garnish. It can take a rather plain or drab-looking beverage and elevate it to dinner party status. A sprig of fresh herbs or a slice of citrus can pique other senses while you are enjoying a drink, by adding both color and aroma to round out the experience.

Toppings also add a punch of flavor to your average drink. You'll find some of my favorite topping options throughout, but mostly for the milkshakes. We'll use both classic Whipped Cream (page 169) as well as Pudding Whipped Cream (page 168), which is more stable, sweeter, and perfect for milkshakes! Dalgona coffee is another topping used in the Cookies 'n' Coffee Milkshake (page 104).

THE FOUNTAIN OF KNOWLEDGE

WHETHER YOU'RE LOOKING TO wind down on the front porch with a glass of lemonade, you're throwing a giant birthday bash, or you're the lucky one hosting the holidays this year, I want you to have all the knowledge you need to whip up these delicious drinks. In this section, I'll share my tips for mixing up all the different drinks in this book, including how to hold your glass while you make a float and how to prevent dilution in your punch recipes. You'll also find that most of the recipes in this book have a notes section, where I've included additional information pertaining to each drink.

One key tip about the recipes in this book is that it's really important to use cold liquids. You'll want to make sure you use chilled sodas, seltzers, juices, coffee, tea, and water in these recipes to prevent the ice from melting too fast and diluting the drinks. I recommend chilling them for at least 1 hour before use. The syrups do not need to be chilled, but should be room temperature before using.

DIRTY SODAS & REFRESHERS

Making dirty sodas is simple and requires very few tools and steps. However, it's important to note that the syrups in these drinks have a higher density than the soda and therefore will want to sit at the bottom of the glass, so it's important to stir well before enjoying.

If you're serving at a party, you'll want to pour the cream directly over nugget or crushed ice to achieve the layered look that makes for a gorgeous presentation. I recommend filling the glass about ½ inch (1.3 cm) below the rim and garnishing, then let guests stir on their own. If you're making one at home for yourself, feel free to add the ingredients all together in no particular order.

These soda recipes were built with what I thought was the best ratio for flavor in that particular drink; however, they are totally customizable if you prefer to add more or less syrup or cream.

Club soda and seltzer are not the same. Club soda is infused with minerals that enhance the flavor and also increase its fizz. Seltzer is relatively plain unless otherwise flavored. Any drinks calling for club soda shouldn't be substituted for seltzer because they need that extra effervescence.

FLOATS & MILKSHAKES

Building a successful float or milkshake really starts with the glass. It's best to use a tall glass, preferably a float or soda glass, or a beer stein, and chill it in the freezer for about 15 minutes before serving.

Make sure to use quality ice cream, usually one that has a 15 percent or more fat content, for both floats and milkshakes. Most frozen yogurts and nondairy ice cream alternatives should also work, but they may not foam as much as traditional hard-serve ice cream because they have a much lower fat content.

When making floats, make sure to pour the soda into the glass slowly at an angle to reduce fizz and risk of overflow.

Then there's the great float debate: Ice cream or soda first? I'm personally a fan of either adding the ice cream first or a combo of both ice cream first and last, but never soda first. Soda is obviously carbonated and when you pour it into the glass, it bubbles up, and those bubbles quickly rise to the surface and pop. So, when you add the ice cream first, the gas molecules in the soda interact with the ingredients in the ice cream, which stabilizes and captures the bubbles and turns them into that velvety foam everyone loves about ice cream floats. If you were to add in the ice cream after pouring your soda, many of the bubbles will have already popped by the time you add the first scoop, so you get less foam. It depends on your preference and whether you like more or less foam.

With that being said, I prefer the finished look of a scoop of ice cream on top of my float, so next time you make one, try adding a scoop or two before pouring the soda, then top it off with one more scoop!

PARTY PUNCHES

Generally speaking, a punch is a mix of fruit juice and a carbonated beverage. So if you have a combination of those two things, you have a punch. Personally, I like to make sure that every punch has at least three different ingredients, and I always include two non-carbonated ingredients, such as fruit juice or lemonade and a soda. The crazy thing about punches is that you can throw a bunch of different ingredients together and most of the time they're delicious!

If you have time, add the non-carbonated ingredients to a pitcher and let them chill in the fridge for 2 hours. This will allow the punch flavors to meld together before serving. This is highly recommended for punches with spices in them. Make sure to add any carbonated ingredients just before serving, for freshness. Even if you don't combine the non-carbonated ingredients in advance, it's still really important to chill the juices and sodas in a punch for at least 1 hour before using, because if you add ice or an ice ring (page 171) to room-temperature ingredients, it's going to melt quicker and dilute the punch more. Speaking of dilution, one of my favorite tricks is to use one of the non-carbonated punch ingredients to make an ice ring or ice cups (page 171), this way as the ice melts it is not impacting the flavor.

Punches can be left plain with fresh fruit to fancy it up or topped with ice cream or sherbet, which gives them a frothy topping similar to that of a soda float. Traditionally, punches are served at parties and these toppings help give them that wow factor in the presentation department.

LEMONADES & ICED TEAS

The best tip I can offer you when making your own lemonade is to clean your fruit well even if the lemons aren't going directly into the drink, as any dirt or residue will cling to the press (see page 20) and potentially end up in the drink with the juice.

For black tea, which is what we'll use in the recipes in this book, you want to prepare it with filtered boiling water. It's also very important that you resist the temptation to squeeze your tea bags after steeping or let them sit too long in the water, as this can cause more tannic acid than desired, which can result in a bitter or sour flavor.

TOOLS YOU'LL NEED

WHEN WORKING ON ANY RECIPE, making sure that you have the tools you need before you start is second only to having all of the ingredients to ensure recipe success. I know that drinks aren't as involved as baking a three-layer cake, but there are still some helpful tools you'll want to have on hand. Many of these are standard items that you likely already have in your kitchen drawers, but some things like muddlers and fine-mesh sieves might be tools you'll want to invest in.

THE BASICS

First and foremost, you're going to need measuring cups and spoons to build these drinks with the proper ratios. It's important to make sure you use a liquid measuring cup to measure ingredients like water, soda, and simple syrup, and a dry measuring cup for ingredients like granulated sugar and cocoa powder.

If you choose to make your syrups at home, you'll need a small saucepan, a whisk, and a fine-mesh sieve.

A cutting board and a chef's knife will come in handy when you need to prep garnishes or halve the lemons for the Roasted Lemonade (page 114). You'll also find that a citrus press will be your new best friend when it comes to making any of the lemonade recipes!

Milkshakes, floats, and some of the punches will require an ice cream scoop. If you don't have one on hand, you can use a 4 oz (120 ml) of ice cream for each scoop that's called for in the recipe.

What you'll need:
* Liquid measuring cup
* Dry measuring cups and spoons
* Saucepan
* Whisk
* Fine-mesh sieve
* Cutting board
* Chef's knife
* Citrus press
* Ice cream scoop

FOR SERVING

You'll need a vessel to serve your drinks in; for most of the dirty sodas you'll want to have highball, collins, or pint glasses, usually around 12 to 16 oz (360 to 420 ml). The refreshers can be served in rocks, highball, or collins glasses, but feel free to use coupe glasses for things like girls' nights, or dinner parties. For the party punches, you'll need either a large bowl and a ladle or a large or small pitcher, and the drinks can be served in whatever glasses you'd like. The floats and milkshakes are going to require larger glasses, preferably soda glasses or beer steins. The teas and lemonades can be served in pretty much any glass. Most recipes will require a straw—make sure to go with wide straws for milkshakes and use more environmentally friendly straw options when possible!

What you'll need:
* Pint glasses
* Collins glasses
* Highball glasses
* Rocks glasses
* Soda glasses or beer steins
* Coupe glasses
* Large punch bowl and ladle
* Small pitcher or carafe
* Large pitcher
* Straws

EXTRAS

There are a few frozen drinks, like the PB & J Milkshake (page 111), that will need a blender. For the Fauxjito (page 77) you'll need a cocktail muddler, which is similar to a pestle but has teeth on the end to help bruise fruit and herbs to release flavor and oils as opposed to crushing completely. A stand or hand mixer and metal mixing bowl will also come in handy, along with some piping bags and tips if you decide to make your own whipped cream. And if you're feeling a little extra and decide to make an ice ring or ice cups, a Bundt pan or cupcake pan is necessary.

What you'll need:
* Blender
* Muddler
* Stand or hand mixer
* Metal mixing bowl
* Piping bags and tips
* Bundt pan or cupcake pan

SETTING THE "NEW" BAR

When you come to a party at my house, chances are you'll find a bowl of punch or a drink bar of some sort. Setting up a drink bar can be as simple or as detailed as you'd like, but there are some key components to include to prepare the best party drink bar.

* Drinkware usually sets the tone for the bar. Go with glass or hard plastic cups if it's for a fancy gathering like a bridal shower, or keep it casual with paper cups for a birthday party.

* Depending on the type of bar you choose to set up, base liquids like soda, hot chocolate, lemonade, tea, or coffee can be served from bowls, pitchers, carafes, or even drink dispensers!

* Optional additions like flavored syrups, juice, and cream can be kept in glass bottles so they're easy to add in. Keep cream or other dairy additions in an ice bucket if it will be out for a while, and even ice cream in a cooler next to the serving station.

* I like to put garnishes and toppings like fresh fruit, whipped cream, and sprinkles in little bowls with small tongs or spoons.

* And finally, don't forget to label everything!

Ultimately, what you're providing and sharing with a drink bar is an experience and the gratification that comes from building and making something yourself. The best part is that it's something the whole family can enjoy.

LIQUID MEASUREMENT CONVERSION TABLE

$1/2$ fl oz	1 tablespoon	15 ml
$3/4$ fl oz	$1^1/_2$ tablespoons	22 ml
1 fl oz	2 tablespoons	30 ml
2 fl oz	$1/4$ cup	60 ml
3 fl oz	6 tablespoons	90 ml
4 fl oz	$1/2$ cup	120 ml
5 fl oz	10 tablespoons	150 ml
6 fl oz	$3/4$ cup	180 ml
8 fl oz	1 cup	240 ml
16 fl oz	2 cups/1 pint	475 ml

DIRTY SODAS

SIMPLE SYRUP MINGLED WITH SODA POP, with or without a splash of cream: that's a dirty soda. This twist on traditional soda is both fun and exciting, with endless flavor possibilities to try. In this chapter, I'm sharing twenty sweet and vivacious recipes that turn a regular old soda into a party in your mouth. These rich, creamy, and refreshing soda beverages are sure to be unlike anything you've ever had before. From unique personal favorites like Breakfast Soda (page 31) and Bohemian Raspberry (page 51), to classics like The OG Dirty Soda (page 24) and Dirty Shirley (page 27), there's guaranteed to be something for everyone!

THE OG DIRTY SODA

SERVES 1

INGREDIENTS

Nugget or crushed ice

8 oz (240 ml) chilled Coke

½ oz (15 ml) Coconut
Simple Syrup (Torani brand)

½ oz (15 ml) freshly squeezed
lime juice

2 oz (60 ml) heavy cream

1 lime slice, for garnish

NOTES

✳ Diet Coke may be used
instead of regular Coke.
Many people also enjoy this
combination with Dr Pepper
instead of Coke, too.

✳ This recipe is also delicious
with a store-bought
sweetened lime juice like
Rose's or Torani's lime syrup.
However, the original is made
with fresh lime juice, which
prevents the drink from being
too heavy and makes it more
on the refreshing side.

Walk into any dirty soda shop and chances are this
combination of Coke, coconut syrup, fresh lime juice,
and cream is at the top of the menu. What might sound
like an odd combination is actually quite refreshing and
less sweet than most of the other dirty soda recipes in
this book or on restaurant menus.

DIRECTIONS

Fill a collins glass halfway with ice.

Pour the Coke, coconut simple syrup, and lime juice
into the glass.

Slowly pour the heavy cream into the glass over
the ice.

Garnish with a lime slice and serve with a straw.
Stir before enjoying.

DIRTY SHIRLEY

SERVES 1

INGREDIENTS

Nugget or crushed ice

6 oz (180 ml) chilled lemon-lime soda or ginger ale

1 to 2 oz (30 to 60 ml) Grenadine Simple Syrup (page 158)

1½ oz (45 ml) heavy cream

1 maraschino cherry, for garnish

1 orange slice, halved, for garnish

1 mint sprig, for garnish

NOTE

＊ I personally prefer to go a little heavy on the grenadine in my Shirley Temples and I use 2 oz (60 ml), but you can use just 1 oz (30 ml) for a less-sweet version.

Shirley Temples were always a treat when I was growing up. This was the "fancy" drink I got to order at restaurants when my family went out, and I still enjoy them to this day. Refreshingly fizzy soda pairs so nicely with the sweet grenadine syrup. And while this might be considered one of the original dirty sodas, it's about to get a little bit dirtier with a splash of heavy cream. And don't forget the maraschino cherries!

DIRECTIONS

Fill a highball glass halfway with ice.

Add in the lemon-lime soda or ginger ale and grenadine syrup.

Top with the heavy cream and garnish with a maraschino cherry, orange slice half, and a sprig of mint. Serve with a straw and stir before enjoying.

MANGO LASSI

SERVES 1

INGREDIENTS

Nugget or crushed ice

4 oz (120 ml) chilled club soda

1 oz (30 ml) Mango
Simple Syrup (page 160)

2 oz (60 ml) heavy cream

Ground cardamom, for topping

3 fresh mango pieces, diced,
for garnish (optional)

1 mint sprig, for garnish
(optional)

NOTE

* The cardamom completes
  the overall experience of
  the drink; I know it might be
  tempting to omit it, but it's
  totally worth it for the extra
  sensory experience.

Inspired by the popular Indian yogurt-based drink,
this recipe blends together club soda, mango syrup,
and cream to create a mildly sweet and fruity
beverage. A dash of cardamom on the top brings all
the components together in a drink that will delight in
both taste and smell.

DIRECTIONS

Fill a double-rocks glass halfway with ice.

Pour the club soda and mango simple syrup into
the glass.

Slowly pour the heavy cream over the top of the ice.

Add a dusting of cardamom.

Garnish with fresh mango pieces and mint, if desired.
Serve with a straw and stir before enjoying.

BREAKFAST SODA

SERVES 1

INGREDIENTS

Coffee Ice Cubes (page 170)

4 oz (120 ml) chilled cream soda

2 oz (60 ml) Cold Brew Coffee
(page 165)

1 oz (30 ml) maple syrup
(see Notes)

2 oz (60 ml) heavy cream
or half-and-half

¼ teaspoon cinnamon sugar,
for topping

NOTES

* A maple-flavored simple syrup
(Torani brand preferred) or a
100% pure maple syrup can
be used in this recipe.

* For a stronger coffee flavor,
use 3 oz (90 ml) each of
coffee and cream soda.

This soda is packed with flavors reminiscent of mornings when you brew your own coffee and take the time to make your favorite syrup-soaked carbs. A base of cream soda and cold brew coffee is sweetened with maple syrup and cream for a drink that will leave you dreaming of a stack of pancakes. Served with coffee ice cubes and a dusting of cinnamon sugar, this glass of sweetness is sure to surprise you—and wake you up!

DIRECTIONS

Fill a highball glass halfway with coffee ice cubes.

Pour in the chilled cream soda, cold brew coffee, and maple syrup.

Gently pour the heavy cream or half-and-half over the ice cubes.

Top with a dusting of cinnamon sugar. Serve with a straw and stir before enjoying.

STRAWBERRIES & CREAM

SERVES 1

INGREDIENTS

Nugget or crushed ice

8 oz (240 ml) chilled strawberry soda (Jarritos or Fanta brand)

½ oz (15 ml) Vanilla Simple Syrup (page 162)

2 oz (60 ml) heavy cream

1 strawberry, for garnish

NOTE

* Classic Simple Syrup (page 158) can be used instead of vanilla.

The sun-ripened sweetness of strawberries and warm vanilla is a classic combination that you just can't go wrong with!

DIRECTIONS

Fill a collins glass halfway with ice.

Pour the strawberry soda and vanilla simple syrup into the glass.

Slowly pour the heavy cream in and garnish with a strawberry. Serve with a straw and stir before enjoying.

DIRTY MULE

SERVES 1

INGREDIENTS

Nugget or crushed ice

7 oz (210 ml) chilled ginger beer
(Fever Tree brand)

1 oz (30 ml) lime syrup
(Torani brand)

2 oz (60 ml) heavy cream

1 lime wedge, for garnish

1 mint sprig, for garnish

NOTE

✳ For a smoother ginger flavor,
feel free to use ginger ale in
this recipe instead.

This twist on a classic Moscow Mule swaps alcohol for
cream in a bold and bubbly recipe. The combination of
creamy, sweet, and spicy is exactly the kind of drink
you want for a Friday night. Each sip has a bit of bite
thanks to a generous amount of ginger beer, but is
balanced out by the lime syrup and heavy cream.

～～～～～～～～～～～～～～～～～

DIRECTIONS

Fill a copper mug or collins glass three-quarters full
with ice.

Pour in the ginger beer and lime syrup.

Slowly pour in the heavy cream.

Garnish with the lime wedge and mint sprig. Serve
with a straw and stir before enjoying.

STRAWBERRY COLADA

SERVES 1

INGREDIENTS

Nugget or crushed ice

8 oz (240 ml) chilled club soda

1 oz (30 ml) Strawberry
Simple Syrup (page 160)

1 oz (30 ml) Pineapple
Simple Syrup (page 160)

½ oz (15 ml) Coconut
Simple Syrup (Torani brand)

2 oz (60 ml) heavy cream

1 pineapple wedge, for garnish

1 strawberry, for garnish

If you like piña coladas, chances are you'll like strawberry ones too! This recipe is one of my personal favorites: I love the fruity island-inspired mash-up of strawberry, pineapple, and coconut syrup. Using club soda instead of a flavored one keeps this drink light while letting the bright fruit flavors shine.

DIRECTIONS

Fill a collins glass halfway with ice.

Pour the club soda and the strawberry, pineapple, and coconut simple syrups into the glass.

Slowly pour the heavy cream over the ice.

Garnish the glass with a pineapple wedge and a strawberry. Serve with a straw and stir before enjoying.

ORANGE DREAM

SERVES 1

INGREDIENTS

Nugget or crushed ice

6 oz (180 ml) chilled orange soda

½ oz (15 ml) Vanilla Simple Syrup
(page 162)

2 oz (60 ml) heavy cream

NOTE

* Classic Simple Syrup (page
  158) can be used instead of
  Vanilla Simple Syrup.

The nostalgia of sun-kissed playgrounds, splash pads, and ice cream trucks is captured in this irresistible soda recipe. There's just something about the way warm and creamy vanilla blends with the juicy and zippy orange in this classic combo that everyone loves!

DIRECTIONS

Fill a highball glass about halfway with ice.

Pour the orange soda and vanilla simple syrup into the glass.

Slowly pour the heavy cream over the ice.

Serve with a straw and stir before enjoying.

ITALIAN CREAM SODA

SERVES 1

INGREDIENTS

Nugget or crushed ice

6 oz (180 ml) chilled club soda

1 to 2 oz (30 to 60 ml)
Fruit Simple Syrup (page 160)

1 oz (30 ml) heavy or light cream

Whipped Cream (page 169),
for topping

1 maraschino cherry, for garnish

NOTES

* Canned whipped cream may
  be used instead of homemade
  whipped cream for topping.

* Because this is just a club
  soda base, the syrup can
  be adjusted for flavor and
  sweetness based on personal
  preference.

* If you want a plain Italian soda,
  skip the heavy cream.

When one of my daughters turned two, we threw a
Two-tti Frutti birthday party for her and had an Italian
soda bar! The kids loved being able to build their own
drinks by choosing their syrup flavors, adding their
soda, and piling on loads of whipped cream, of course.
I think this is such a fun addition to any gathering and
it's so easy to set one up.

DIRECTIONS

Fill a collins glass halfway with ice.

Pour the club soda and syrup into the glass.

Slowly pour in the heavy or light cream, making sure to
leave about a ½ in (1.3 cm) of room between the drink
and the top of the glass.

Pipe on the whipped cream and top with a
maraschino cherry.

ROCKET POP

SERVES 1

INGREDIENTS

1½ oz (45 ml) Grenadine Simple Syrup (page 158)

Nugget or crushed ice

½ oz (15 ml) freshly squeezed lime juice

5 oz (150 ml) chilled berry lemonade soda (Jones brand)

2 oz (60 ml) heavy cream

This recipe is inspired by the original Bomb Pop popsicle and is perfect for serving to friends and family on the Fourth of July. A three-layered red, white, and blue drink that would take anyone back to hot summer days chasing down the ice cream truck, cannonballs in the pool, and sparklers at sunset. It's a nostalgic yet still relevant treat, now in soda pop form!

DIRECTIONS

Pour the grenadine simple syrup into a collins glass.

Add the ice to the glass.

Pour the lime juice and berry lemonade soda over the ice.

Then slowly pour in the heavy cream.

Serve with a straw and stir before enjoying.

NOTES

* It is best to use nugget ice or crushed ice in this recipe to help support the layers.

* This three-layered soda should be stirred before drinking for the best experience, since the syrup will sit on the bottom of the glass. In order to have clear layers for presentation, it's important to follow the directions and order of the ingredients exactly.

* Any red simple syrup can be used; I also love this with cherry, strawberry, and raspberry flavors (see page 160).

CARAMEL APPLE LOLLIPOP

INGREDIENTS

Ice cubes

8 oz (240 ml) chilled
green apple soda (Jones brand)

1½ oz (45 ml) Salted Caramel
Simple Syrup (Torani brand)

NOTE

✳ Caramel syrup may be used
  instead of salted caramel.

This one is for my fellow millennials who went crazy
for those green apple lollipops dipped in caramel
growing up. Every fall when those babies hit the
shelves, it was the unofficial marker that the season
had arrived. I remember hoarding and hiding them to
make sure my brother didn't get his hands on them—
they were basically gold. And this drink is too!

DIRECTIONS

Fill a double-rocks glass halfway with ice.

Pour the green apple soda and salted caramel simple
syrup into the glass.

Serve with a straw and stir before enjoying.

TWILIGHT SWIM

SERVES 1

INGREDIENTS

Nugget or crushed ice

8 oz (240 ml) chilled
lemon-lime soda

1 oz (30 ml) Raspberry
Simple Syrup (page 160)

1 oz (30 ml) Peach
Simple Syrup (page 160)

½ oz (30 ml) Vanilla
Simple Syrup (page 162)

1½ oz (45 ml) heavy cream

1 peach slice, for garnish

There's nothing quite like an evening swim after a balmy summer day of stuffing your face with peach cobbler and barbecued chicken. The water is warm but refreshing and the reds and oranges of the sun's descent glitter across the surface. This drink is inspired by those perfect summer nights, with a refreshing base of lemon-lime soda mixed with the flavors of juicy raspberries, ripe peaches, sweet vanilla, and a splash of cream.

DIRECTIONS

Fill a pint glass halfway with ice.

Pour the lemon-lime soda and the raspberry, peach, and vanilla simple syrups into the glass.

Slowly pour the heavy cream directly over the ice.

Garnish with a peach slice. Serve with a straw and stir before enjoying.

SOUTHERN DELIGHT

SERVES 1

INGREDIENTS

Nugget or crushed ice

10 oz (300 ml) chilled Dr Pepper

1½ oz (45 ml) Peach Simple Syrup (page 160)

2 oz (60 ml) heavy cream

1 peach slice, for garnish

This soda is as sweet as the South, thanks to the Dr Pepper and peach syrup! It has a truly dynamic flavor profile that tastes like a slightly fruity iced coffee.

~~~~~~

DIRECTIONS

Fill a collins or highball glass halfway with ice.

Pour the Dr Pepper and peach syrup into the glass.

Slowly pour the heavy cream over the ice.

Garnish with a peach slice. Serve with a straw and stir before enjoying.

BOHEMIAN RASPBERRY

SERVES 1

INGREDIENTS

Nugget or crushed ice

8 oz (240 ml) chilled Dr Pepper

1 oz (30 ml) Raspberry
Simple Syrup (page 160)

½ oz (15 ml) Coconut
Simple Syrup (Torani brand)

2 oz (60 ml) heavy cream

Raspberries, for garnish
(optional)

Dr Pepper is my go-to when a fountain soda craving strikes, but this dirty soda recipe may have ruined it forever because now I'll probably always need it to have a splash of raspberry and coconut simple syrups. This drink is an absolutely delicious and unexpected combination of flavors that I just can't get enough of!

DIRECTIONS

Fill a collins glass halfway with ice.

Pour the Dr Pepper and the raspberry and coconut simple syrups into the glass.

Slowly pour the heavy cream over the top of the ice.

Garnish with fresh raspberries if desired. Serve with a straw and stir before enjoying.

BOARDWALK SUNSET

SERVES 1

INGREDIENTS

Ice cubes

6 oz (180 ml) chilled orange soda

½ oz (15 ml) Pineapple Simple Syrup (page 160)

½ oz (15 ml) Strawberry Simple Syrup (page 160)

½ oz (15 ml) Raspberry Simple Syrup (page 160)

1 orange slice, for garnish

1 strawberry, for garnish

NOTE

* If you love this drink but prefer less sweetness, use 3 oz (90 ml) of orange soda and 3 oz (90 ml) of club soda.

This dirty soda is probably the sweetest in the book. It's made without cream and loaded with four different fruit flavors: raspberry, strawberry, orange, and pineapple. This drink is like a snow cone after all the ice has melted and you're left with one last super-sweet sip at the bottom.

DIRECTIONS

Fill a highball glass halfway with ice.

Pour the orange soda and pineapple, strawberry, and raspberry simple syrups into the glass.

Garnish with an orange slice and a strawberry. Serve with a straw and stir before enjoying.

BUTTERBEER

INGREDIENTS

Nugget or crushed ice

6 oz (180 ml) chilled cream soda

1 oz (30 ml) Salted Caramel Simple Syrup (Torani brand)

1 oz (30 ml) Butterscotch Simple Syrup (Torani brand)

1/4 teaspoon butter extract

1 1/2 oz (45 ml) heavy cream

1/2 cup (120 ml) Pudding Whipped Cream (page 168)

Caramel sauce, for topping

Sprinkles, for topping (optional)

Hey, Muggles! Grab your mugs, it's butterbeer time! You won't even need a house elf to prepare this magical beverage for you because it's so easy to make at home with cream soda, caramel and butterscotch syrups, butter extract, and cream!

DIRECTIONS

Fill a pint-sized glass mug about halfway with ice.

Pour the cream soda, salted caramel and butterscotch simple syrups, and butter extract into the mug.

Slowly pour in the heavy cream over the ice.

Pipe the whipped cream on top of the heavy cream.

Drizzle with caramel sauce and top with sprinkles, if desired. Serve with a straw and stir before enjoying.

NOTES

* Regular Whipped Cream (page 169) or canned whipped cream may be used instead of pudding whipped cream for topping.

* Adding the butter extract really makes the butterscotch flavor pop in this drink. It's generally found near the other flavor extracts in the baking aisle at the supermarket.

* I prefer using vanilla-flavored pudding whipped cream, but white chocolate, cheesecake, caramel, or butterscotch are all great choices to pair with this soda recipe. Just note that the latter two flavors will make beige-colored whipped cream instead of white.

CAULDRON BUBBLES

SERVES 1

INGREDIENTS

1 oz (30 ml) Pineapple
Simple Syrup (page 160)

1 drop black gel food coloring

Nugget or crushed ice

6 oz (180 ml) chilled
green apple soda (Jones brand)

2 oz (60 ml) heavy cream

1 drop purple gel food coloring

NOTES

* Traditional food coloring may
  be used as an alternative to gel
  food coloring, but you will need
  5 or 6 drops of food coloring to
  reach a similar color intensity
  as the gel colors.

* Nugget or crushed ice is best
  to help support the layers.

* In order to have clear
  layers for presentation,
  it's important to follow the
  directions and order of
  the ingredients exactly.

This colorful concoction looks like it came straight from
a witch's cauldron! A flavor mash-up of green apple
soda, pineapple syrup, and a touch of cream will leave
all the little goblins and houseguests wanting more.

DIRECTIONS

In a collins or highball glass, mix together the pineapple
syrup and black gel food coloring.

Add ice on top of the syrup.

Slowly pour in the green apple soda.

In a small measuring cup, mix together the heavy
cream and purple gel food coloring, then pour the
mixture over the top of the soda.

Serve with a straw and stir before enjoying.

BLACK FOREST

SERVES 1

INGREDIENTS

Nugget or crushed ice

8 oz (240 ml) chilled Dr Pepper

2 oz (60 ml) Cherry
Simple Syrup (page 160)

1 oz (30 ml) Chocolate
Simple Syrup (page 164)

2 oz (60 ml) heavy cream

Whipped Cream (page 169)

1 fresh black cherry, for garnish

NOTE

* Make sure to use a chocolate
syrup like my recipe on page
164 or Hershey's chocolate
syrup, not a chocolate-flavored
simple syrup.

I know dirty soda recipes are sweet by nature, but
this one is pure dessert! An indulgent treat inspired
by the popular German cake recipe, this drink
combines the twenty-three flavors of Dr Pepper with
cherry and chocolate. The heavy cream and whipped
cream give it an impressive finish with a cherry on top!

DIRECTIONS

Fill a highball glass halfway with ice.

Pour the Dr Pepper and cherry and chocolate simple
syrups into the glass.

Slowly pour the heavy cream over the top of the ice.

Top with whipped cream and garnish with a cherry.
Serve with a straw and stir before enjoying.

AMERICAN PIE

SERVES 1

INGREDIENTS

Nugget or crushed ice

12 oz (360 ml) blueberry soda (Eli brand)

1 oz (30 ml) Apple Simple Syrup (page 160)

½ oz (15 ml) Shortbread Simple Syrup (Torani brand)

¼ oz (7.5 ml) Brown Sugar Cinnamon Simple Syrup (page 159)

2 oz (60 ml) heavy cream

¼ teaspoon cinnamon sugar, for topping

This is such a fun soda. Made with a blueberry base and apple syrup, this tastes like a late New England summer. The shortbread syrup gives it a hint of buttery crust flavor while the cinnamon adds a tiny spark of spice. And the cream on top, well, that just elevates the drink to à la mode status.

DIRECTIONS

Fill a pint glass halfway with ice.

Pour the blueberry soda and the apple, shortbread, and brown sugar cinnamon simple syrups into the glass.

Slowly pour the heavy cream over the ice.

Dust the top with cinnamon sugar. Serve with a straw and stir before enjoying.

SANTA BABY

SERVES 1

INGREDIENTS

2 oz (60 ml) Strawberry
Simple Syrup (page 160)

Nugget or crushed ice

8 oz (240 ml) chilled
green apple soda (Jones brand)

2 oz (60 ml) heavy cream

Skip the milk and serve the big guy a glass of ice-cold
dirty soda with those cookies this year. Layers of red,
green, and white make for a cheery holiday drink
that's bursting with sweet strawberry and tart green
apple flavors!

DIRECTIONS

Pour the strawberry simple syrup into a collins or
highball glass.

Add the ice on top of the syrup.

Slowly pour in the green apple soda over the ice.

Then slowly pour in the heavy cream.

Serve with a straw and stir before enjoying.

NOTES

* If you prefer a less fruity flavor, swap the strawberry
  syrup out for caramel and a couple of drops of red
  gel food coloring for a creamy caramel apple drink.

* It's best to use nugget ice or crushed ice in this
  recipe to help support the layers.

* This three-layered soda should be stirred before
  drinking for the best experience since the syrup will
  sit on the bottom of the glass. In order to have clear
  layers for presentation, it's important to follow the
  directions and order of the ingredients exactly.

SPRITZERS & REFRESHERS

CHANGE CAN BE SO REFRESHING. And let's face it, between the soda, the syrup, and the cream, dirty sodas are a little on the heavy side. With the rise in popularity of soda water and seltzer, it seemed fitting to give them their own little section in this book for balance. These drinks use either club soda or seltzer instead of traditional soda, and they eliminate the cream, resulting in lighter-tasting beverages. But don't worry, they don't lack in fun or flavor—each one is still unique, delicious, and worthy of a spot at the table!

RASPBERRY LIME RICKEY

SERVES 1

INGREDIENTS

Ice cubes

1 oz (30 ml) freshly squeezed lime juice

2 oz (60 ml) Raspberry Simple Syrup (page 160)

5 oz (150 ml) chilled club soda

3 lime slices, for garnish

Raspberries, for garnish (optional)

NOTES

✳ Strawberry, blackberry, or cherry simple syrup can be used in place of raspberry.

✳ Make this float-style with a scoop of raspberry sorbet!

This is for my Great-Nana Jackie, who spent her summers in the '90s driving my nana, my brother, and me to campgrounds and diners around New England. Although we were pretty cute, and I'm sure she loved the time she spent with us, I secretly think she did it just to get her Lime Rickey fix!

~~~~~~~~~~

DIRECTIONS

Fill a double-rocks glass most of the way with ice.

Pour the lime juice and raspberry syrup into the glass.

Top with the club soda.

Garnish with 3 lime slices and some raspberries, if desired. Serve with a straw and stir before enjoying.

COFFEE SODA

SERVES 1

INGREDIENTS

Ice or Coffee Ice Cubes
(page 170)

8 oz (240 ml) Cold Brew Coffee
(page 165)

3 oz (90 ml) chilled club soda

NOTE

* Feel free to also add your
favorite flavored simple
syrup—a little goes a long
way in this recipe.

If you're looking to cut back on your expensive iced
coffee habit, this is the soda for you. A refreshing mix
of cold brew and club soda over ice offers a delightfully
caffeinated beverage with a light, sophisticated, and
almost fruity flavor.

~~~~~~

DIRECTIONS

Fill a pint glass with ice or coffee ice cubes.

Pour the coffee and club soda into the glass.

Serve with a straw and stir before enjoying.

ISLAND BREEZE

SERVES 1

INGREDIENTS

Ice cubes

8 oz (240 ml) chilled
pineapple seltzer

½ oz (15 ml) Lime Simple Syrup
(Torani brand)

½ oz (15 ml) Coconut
Simple Syrup (Torani brand)

1 pineapple wedge, for garnish

1 lime slice, for garnish

I've got two tickets to paradise. Just kidding, I don't actually, but I do have pineapple seltzer and I'm going to add it to some lime and coconut syrups and pretend it's the same thing. I highly recommend pairing this drink with a Hawaiian shirt for the full experience.

DIRECTIONS

Fill a double-rocks glass halfway with ice.

Pour the pineapple seltzer and lime and coconut simple syrups into the glass.

Garnish with a pineapple wedge and a lime slice. Serve with a straw and stir before enjoying.

MOM JUICE

SERVES 1

INGREDIENTS

Ice cubes

4 oz (120 ml) chilled
vanilla seltzer (Polar brand)

3 oz (90 ml) 100%
pomegranate juice
(POM brand)

½ oz (15 ml) Vanilla
Simple Syrup (page 162)

½ tablespoon fresh
pomegranate arils,
for garnish (optional)

Inspired by my mom, this is the perfect light and fizzy
drink for a Mother's Day brunch! The vanilla adds
strong notes of warmth and sweetness, while the
pomegranate juice lends a firm fruity flavor that is so
delightful that every mom will love it!

~~~~~~~~~~~~~~~~~~~~~~~~~~~~~~

DIRECTIONS

Fill a collins glass halfway with ice.

Pour the vanilla seltzer, pomegranate juice, and vanilla
simple syrup into the glass. Stir to combine.

Garnish with pomegranate arils, if desired, and serve
with a straw.

BLUEBERRY LAVENDER SPRITZER

SERVES 1

INGREDIENTS

Nugget or crushed ice

5 oz (150 ml) chilled club soda

1 oz (15 ml) Blueberry
Simple Syrup (page 160)

1 oz (15 ml) Lavender
Simple Syrup (page 163)

1 lavender sprig, for garnish

1 blueberry, for garnish

The smooth mix of blueberry and lavender was
inspired by late July, when both are in season in New
England and every balmy night calls for a crisp, light,
and refreshing beverage to sip on. This drink is mild,
delightful, and sophisticated and it's a sure winner for
showers, brunch, and girls' nights.

DIRECTIONS

Fill a coupe glass halfway with ice.

Pour the club soda and blueberry and lavender simple
syrups into the glass.

Stir and garnish with a lavender sprig and a blueberry.

FAUXJITO

SERVES 1

INGREDIENTS

10 fresh mint leaves

3 lime wedges

1½ oz (45 ml) freshly squeezed
lime juice (1½ limes)

1 oz (30 ml) Classic
Simple Syrup (page 158)

Nugget or crushed ice

4 oz (120 ml) chilled club soda

1 mint sprig, for garnish

NOTES

* This recipe has a strong lime
  flavor, so feel free to reduce
  the amount of ice slightly and
  add a little more club soda if
  you want a lighter flavor.

* For an extra fruity twist, use
  a fruit-flavored syrup like
  strawberry, raspberry, or
  pineapple (page 160) instead
  of classic simple syrup.

* A lime has about 1 oz (30 ml)
  of juice in it. To get the most
  juice out of your limes, roll
  them between your palm and
  the counter before slicing
  and juicing.

Expectant mamas, this one is for you! This is the drink
I used to hide my pregnancies before we were ready
to share our news with friends and family. Trust me,
having what looks like a classic mojito in hand is sure
to keep everyone from finding out until you're ready to
reveal the big news. So my husband became a Fauxjito
master, finding the perfect ratio of fresh mint and limes,
simple syrup, and club soda. I still crave them to this
day and often opt for them over traditional cocktails
because of how flavorful and refreshing they are. Oh,
and the best part—one of these effervescent drinks is
less than 70 calories!

DIRECTIONS

In a collins glass, use a muddler to muddle the mint
leaves and lime wedges to release the juice and oils.
Leave the wedges and leaves in the glass.

Pour in the lime juice and simple syrup.

Fill the glass almost full of ice.

Pour in the club soda.

Slap the sprig of mint between your palms to release
its oils and place it in the glass right next to a straw.
Stir before enjoying.

MANGO BERRY SPLASH

SERVES 1

INGREDIENTS

Ice cubes

4 oz (120 ml) chilled
raspberry seltzer (Bubly brand)

½ oz (15 ml) Mango
Simple Syrup (page 160)

½ oz (15ml) Strawberry
Simple Syrup (page 160)

1 mango slice, for garnish

NOTE

* Strawberry seltzer can be
  used in place of raspberry
  seltzer in this recipe.

Inspired by my daughters' summer babysitters—who
drank more berry seltzer and ate more mangoes than
I could keep up with—here's a riveting combination of
sweet mango and juicy berries that's light and bubbly.

DIRECTIONS

Fill a double-rocks glass halfway with ice.

Pour the seltzer and mango and strawberry simple
syrups into the glass.

Garnish with a slice of mango. Serve with a straw and
stir before enjoying.

BALSAMIC FIZZ

SERVES 1

INGREDIENTS

Ice cubes

7 oz (210 ml) chilled
strawberry seltzer

½ oz (15 ml) Classic
Simple Syrup (page 158)

½ oz (15 ml) freshly squeezed
lemon juice

½ tablespoon balsamic vinegar

1 lemon wedge

1 strawberry, for garnish

I know what you're thinking: vinegar? Yes, vinegar. Fizzy vinegar-based drinks, also known as shrubs, are making a comeback. And rightfully so, they're zingy, refreshing, and absolutely packed with flavor. A touch of vinegar goes a long way and a bit of simple syrup and fresh lemon juice help maintain balance, while strawberry seltzer tops off this brilliantly carbonated drink. It is lovely for backyard BBQs and dinner parties alike!

DIRECTIONS

Fill a double-rocks glass with ice.

Pour the seltzer, simple syrup, lemon juice, and balsamic vinegar into the glass.

Gently squeeze the lemon wedge into the glass before dropping it in, then garnish with a strawberry. Serve with a straw and stir before enjoying.

NOTES

* You can also enjoy this recipe with strawberry simple syrup (page 160) instead of classic simple syrup to highlight the strawberry flavor of the seltzer.

* Feel free to experiment with some artisanal fruity-flavored vinegars or other seltzer flavors in this drink, such as raspberry, pomegranate, or cherry.

BLACKBERRY BRAMBLE

SERVES 1

INGREDIENTS

Ice cubes

6 oz (180 ml) chilled
blackberry seltzer (Bubly brand)

1 oz (30 ml) Blackberry
Simple Syrup (page 160)

½ oz (15 ml) freshly squeezed
lemon juice

2 lemon slices, for garnish

1 blackberry, for garnish

Is it just me or is the blackberry a totally underrated fruit? I have such fond memories of picking ripe wild blackberries as a kid and selling them at our little country store. I guess you could say that was my first taste of being an entrepreneur. These days, I'll make a batch of blackberry simple syrup each season and enjoy its deep and complex flavor in spritzers and lemonades until the end of summer. This bramble is one of those drinks, brightened with a bit of fresh lemon juice and topped with blackberry seltzer.

~~~~~~~~~~~~~~~~~~~~~~~~~~

DIRECTIONS

Fill a double-rocks glass about halfway with ice.

Pour the seltzer, blackberry simple syrup, and lemon juice into the glass.

Stir and garnish with lemon slices and a blackberry. Serve with a straw.

WINTER SPRITZER

SERVES 1

INGREDIENTS

Ice cubes

2 oz (60 ml) chilled 100% unsweetened cranberry juice (Ocean Spray Pure brand)

½ oz (15 ml) Lime Simple Syrup (Torani brand)

4 oz (120 ml) chilled lime seltzer

7 cranberries, for garnish

1 lime slice, for garnish

NOTE

* The flavor profile of this drink is a bit on the tarter side. You can increase the lime simple syrup to 1 oz (30 ml) for added sweetness if you prefer.

This tart yet refreshing drink is a light alternative to the typical sugary beverages of the holidays. It has a subtle note of sweetness to balance the cranberry and lime, while maintaining that bright punch of flavor.

DIRECTIONS

Fill a double-rocks glass halfway with ice.

Pour the cranberry juice, lime simple syrup, and lime seltzer into the glass. Stir to combine.

Garnish with cranberries and a slice of lime and serve with a straw.

FLOATS & MILKSHAKES

FLOATS STARTED AS A CULINARY IMPROVISATION and are now an American classic. Did you know that floats were invented unintentionally on a hot summer day in the 1870s? A soda jerk ran out of ice and decided to use ice cream to keep the soda cold instead, giving us a most beautiful gift: the ice cream soda float. For over a hundred years, soda and vanilla ice cream have been the ultimate drink for dessert, and I personally like to go a little heavy on the ice cream for an extra creamy float. And since we're on the topic of frozen things, I thought it would be fun to add some milkshakes to the mix as well.

ROOT BEER FLOAT

SERVES 1

INGREDIENTS

4 scoops vanilla ice cream, divided

12 oz (360 ml) chilled root beer (Hank or IBC brand)

NOTE

✳ Chill your glass in the freezer for 15 minutes before use for best results.

It's a classic for a reason. In the summer, my family and I sometimes make floats instead of having regular ice cream for dessert, and let me tell you, my middle child can down a Root Beer Float without spilling a drop. Somehow, she's not as skilled with a small cup of water, but I guess that just goes to show how much she loves them.

DIRECTIONS

Add 2 scoops of the vanilla ice cream to a large beer mug or soda glass.

Hold the mug at a slight angle and slowly pour in the root beer, making sure it doesn't foam over the edge of the glass.

Top off the glass with the remaining 2 scoops ice cream and serve with a straw.

LEMONADE FLOAT

SERVES 1

INGREDIENTS

1 scoop vanilla ice cream

6 oz (180 ml) chilled
Roasted Lemonade (page 114)

2 oz (60 ml) chilled
lemon-lime soda

1 lemon slice, for garnish

NOTES

* Chill your glass in the freezer
  for 15 minutes before use for
  best results.

* Regular lemonade may be
  used in this recipe, just be
  sure it's sweetened so that it
  isn't too tart and pairs nicely
  with the vanilla ice cream.

A mix of bright lemonade and dreamy vanilla ice cream
topped with soda is the best of summer in one drink!
It's for those moments when you can't quite choose
between quenching your thirst and satisfying your
sweet tooth.

DIRECTIONS

Add the scoop of ice cream to a collins or soda glass.

Slowly pour in the lemonade and lemon-lime soda,
making sure it doesn't foam over the rim of the glass.

Garnish with a lemon slice and serve with a straw.

BROWN COW FLOAT

SERVES 1

INGREDIENTS

½ to 1 oz (15 to 30 ml) Chocolate Simple Syrup (page 164), plus more for topping

3 scoops vanilla ice cream

6 oz (180 ml) chilled cola or root beer

Whipped Cream (page 169), for topping

1 maraschino cherry, for garnish

Sprinkles, for garnish

NOTES

✳ Chill your glass in the freezer for 15 minutes before use for best results.

✳ Canned whipped cream may be used instead of homemade whipped cream for topping.

A Brown Cow is considered one of the classic floats; however, people have a lot of different opinions about the ingredients. But a few things are certain: It's made with chocolate syrup, ice cream, and cola. Whether you choose chocolate or vanilla ice cream is up to you. And even though many will argue which cola they think should be used, I say pick your favorite!

DIRECTIONS

Drizzle the chocolate syrup around the inside of a soda glass.

Add the scoops of ice cream to the glass.

Slowly pour in the cola or root beer, making sure it doesn't foam over the rim of the glass.

Top with whipped cream and drizzle with more chocolate syrup, then garnish with a maraschino cherry and sprinkles. Serve with a wide straw.

PINEAPPLE ORANGE FLOAT

SERVES 1

INGREDIENTS

2 scoops vanilla ice cream

6 oz (180 ml) chilled orange soda

3 oz (90 ml) chilled pineapple juice

NOTE

 Chill your glass in the freezer for 15 minutes before use for best results.

A classic orange soda float gets a much-needed upgrade with the addition of pineapple juice. The acidity of the juice helps cut the sweetness of the soda and adds a tropical twist of flavor that pairs really nicely with vanilla ice cream.

DIRECTIONS

Add the vanilla ice cream to a pint or soda glass.

Hold the glass at a slight angle and slowly pour in the orange soda and pineapple juice so they don't foam over the rim of the glass.

Serve with a straw.

SHIRLEY TEMPLE FLOAT

SERVES 1

INGREDIENTS

3 scoops vanilla ice cream, divided

1 oz (30 ml) Grenadine Simple Syrup (page 158)

6 oz (180 ml) chilled ginger ale or lemon-lime soda

Maraschino cherries, for garnish

1 lime slice, for garnish

NOTE

* Chill your glass in the freezer for 15 minutes before use for best results.

This float recipe is basically two vintage soda drinks in one! This easy three-ingredient recipe is made with a Shirley Temple base of grenadine syrup, ginger ale or lemon-lime soda, and scoops of vanilla ice cream for a light yet creamy soda float. Add extras like maraschino cherries and sliced limes for a fancy finish.

DIRECTIONS

Add 2 scoops of the vanilla ice cream and the grenadine syrup to a soda glass.

Holding the glass at a slight angle, pour in the ginger ale or lemon-lime soda.

Add the remaining scoop vanilla ice cream.

Garnish with maraschino cherries and a lime slice. Serve with a straw and stir well before enjoying.

CHOCOLATE MILK FLOAT

SERVES 1

INGREDIENTS

8 oz (240 ml) whole milk

2 oz (60 ml) Chocolate Simple Syrup (page 164), plus more for topping

2 scoops chocolate ice cream

4 oz (120 ml) chilled club soda

NOTES

✳ Chill your glass in the freezer for 15 minutes before use for best results.

✳ You can use 10 oz (300 ml) of store-bought chocolate milk instead of the syrup and whole milk if you prefer.

✳ Vanilla ice cream is also fairly common to use in a chocolate milk float if you want to mix it up a little—substitute it for the chocolate ice cream in the recipe.

This is such a great float for kiddos! Since it's made with milk and club soda, it's lower in sugar than the other frozen drink recipes in this book, but still fun and bubbly. Letting the kids stir together the chocolate syrup and milk and scoop their own ice cream gives them a sense of accomplishment and independence. And when you add the club soda—it's as exciting as a paper-mache volcano, if not more so because they get to eat it!

DIRECTIONS

Pour the milk and chocolate simple syrup into a soda glass and stir.

Add the ice cream to the glass and slowly top up with club soda.

Drizzle with more chocolate simple syrup and serve with a straw.

COCONUT LIME SHERBET FLOAT

SERVES 1

INGREDIENTS

2 scoops lime sherbet

½ oz (15 ml) Coconut
Simple Syrup (Torani brand)

½ oz (15 ml) freshly squeezed
lime juice

2 oz (60 ml) chilled
pineapple juice

5 oz (150 ml) chilled
lemon-lime soda

1 lime wedge, for garnish

NOTE

* Chill your glass in the freezer
  for 15 minutes before use for
  best results.

This fruity float packs a punch of lime mingled
with pineapple and coconut flavors. The
sherbet creates a velvety smooth froth that kids
will absolutely love.

DIRECTIONS

Add the sherbet to a collins or soda glass.

Pour the coconut simple syrup and lime and pineapple
juices into the glass.

Hold the glass at a slight angle and pour in the
lemon-lime soda, being careful that the foam doesn't
rise over the rim of the glass.

Stir and garnish with a lime wedge and serve
with a straw.

PURPLE COW FLOAT

SERVES 1

INGREDIENTS

2 scoops vanilla ice cream

8 oz (240 ml) chilled grape soda

NOTES

* Chill your glass in the freezer for 15 minutes before use for best results.

* This float recipe is also commonly made with sparkling grape juice.

For my mother-in-law and all the other grape soda lovers, this one's for you. An ultra-sweet mix of grape soda and vanilla ice cream makes this drink a classic.

DIRECTIONS

Add the vanilla ice cream to a soda glass.

Hold the glass at a slight angle and slowly pour in the grape soda, making sure it doesn't foam up over the rim of the glass.

Serve with a straw.

COOKIES 'N' COFFEE MILKSHAKE

SERVES 1

INGREDIENTS

1 oz (30 ml) hot water

2 tablespoons granulated sugar

1 tablespoon instant coffee granules

4 scoops coffee ice cream

5 Oreos or chocolate sandwich cookies, divided

4 oz (120 ml) whole milk

NOTE

＊ While dalgona coffee is my go-to topping for this milkshake, you can use Whipped Cream (page 169), Pudding Whipped Cream (page 168), or canned whipped cream instead.

I'm willing to bet once you've tried this milkshake, you'll want to start dipping Oreos and other chocolate sandwich cookies into your morning latte.

DIRECTIONS

Place your milkshake glass in the freezer for 15 minutes while you prepare the recipe in the blender.

In a medium bowl, prepare the coffee topping (dalgona coffee) by beating together the hot water, sugar, and instant coffee until pale, thick, and foamy, for about 2 minutes, preferably with a handheld mixer fitted with 1 beater.

Add the ice cream, 4 of the sandwich cookies, and the whole milk to a blender and blend until smooth for 20 to 30 seconds.

Pour the mixture into the chilled milkshake glass. Top with the coffee topping.

Garnish with the remaining sandwich cookie and serve with a wide straw.

BIRTHDAY CAKE MILKSHAKE

SERVES 1

INGREDIENTS

Vanilla Pudding Whipped Cream (page 168) or regular Whipped Cream (page 169), for topping

5 scoops vanilla ice cream

4 oz (120 ml) whole milk

½ cup (132 g) white frosting (Pillsbury brand), plus more for the rim of the glass (optional)

2 tablespoons sprinkles, plus more for topping

1 mini cupcake, for garnish

Birthday candles, for garnish

NOTES

* Make a chocolate cake version by using chocolate ice cream and frosting and adding 2 oz (60 ml) of Chocolate Simple Syrup (page 164).

* You can purchase mini cupcakes at your local supermarket or your favorite bakery.

Make a wish and blow out the candle on this fun birthday cake alternative! In this recipe, a classic vanilla milkshake is blended with some of that super-sweet store-bought frosting to make it taste just like a birthday cake. You can easily make a chocolate version too!

DIRECTIONS

Place your milkshake glass in the freezer for 15 minutes while you prepare the recipe in the blender.

If using pudding whipped cream, prepare the cream before the milkshake.

Add the ice cream, milk, and frosting to a blender and pulse until smooth. Fold in the sprinkles.

You can spread 2 more tablespoons of frosting around the edge of the glass and coat in more sprinkles, if desired.

Pour the mixture into the chilled milkshake glass.

Top with the whipped cream, additional sprinkles, and a mini cupcake.

Don't forget a birthday candle on top of the mini cupcake!

MALTED CHOCOLATE MILKSHAKE

SERVES 1

INGREDIENTS

Whipped cream (page 169), for topping

4 scoops chocolate ice cream

6 oz (180 ml) chocolate milk

¼ cup (31 g) malted milk powder

Chocolate Simple Syrup (page 164), for topping

Sprinkles, for garnish

1 maraschino cherry, for garnish

NOTE

* A vanilla version can be made by using vanilla ice cream and plain whole milk instead of chocolate milk.

One of my fondest memories from childhood is going to breakfast with my dad at The Coffee Shop, because breakfast always included a malted chocolate milkshake for us to split. It was served in a giant metal cup—thick, cold, and insanely delicious. As a kid, this made him the coolest dad ever; now, as a parent myself, I wonder what he was thinking! But every now and then I order or make one just so I can feel like a kid again.

DIRECTIONS

Place your milkshake glass in the freezer for 15 minutes while you prepare the recipe in the blender.

If making your own whipped cream, prepare the cream before the milkshake.

Add the ice cream, milk, and malted milk powder to a blender and blend until smooth.

Pour the mixture into the chilled milkshake glass.

Top with whipped cream, chocolate simple syrup, sprinkles, and a maraschino cherry.

PB & J MILKSHAKE

SERVES 1

INGREDIENTS

Vanilla Pudding Whipped Cream (page 168) or regular Whipped Cream (page 169)

3 scoops strawberry ice cream

4 oz (240 ml) whole milk

¼ cup (60 g) creamy peanut butter, plus more for the rim of the glass (optional)

2 tablespoons raspberry jam, plus more for topping

Pinch salt

Chopped nuts, for topping

Mini PB & J sandwich, for topping (optional)

NOTES

* Strawberry jam or grape jelly can be used instead of raspberry jam.

* To make your mini sandwiches for the garnish, you can cut a traditional PB & J sandwich into quarters or use a mini uncrustable or round biscuit cutter.

A tribute to childhood, this milkshake is everyone's favorite (or maybe loathed) lunchbox meal in frozen form! There's an ongoing debate in my family about what jelly should be used in a peanut butter and jelly sandwich—I'm team raspberry or strawberry—but if you're a grape fan and want to use that instead, I won't judge you too harshly. Either way, this milkshake tastes just like a PB & J, but better!

DIRECTIONS

Place your milkshake glass in the freezer for 15 minutes while you prepare the recipe in the blender.

If using pudding whipped cream, prepare it before the milkshake.

Add the ice cream, milk, peanut butter, raspberry jam, and salt to a blender and pulse until smooth.

You can spread more tablespoons of peanut butter around the edge of the glass and coat in chopped nuts, if desired.

Pour the mixture into the chilled milkshake glass.

Top with the whipped cream, raspberry jam, chopped nuts, and a mini PB & J sandwich, if desired. Serve with a straw.

LEMONADES & ICED TEAS

LEMONADE AND ICED TEA are pretty much my drinks of choice in the summer, and I love shaking them up with new and unique flavors. From their humble origins along the Mediterranean Coast and the World's Fair to the sidewalk stands of America's suburbs, it's safe to say these two ice-cold beverages are a favorite among many. This chapter has a tantalizing mix of classic recipes and fresh takes that will have your taste buds begging for more!

ROASTED LEMONADE

SERVES 4

INGREDIENTS

1 to 1¼ cups (240 ml to 300 ml) Roasted Lemon Juice (page 167, see Notes)

1 cup (240 ml) Classic Simple Syrup (page 158)

4 cups (960 ml) cold filtered water

1 lemon, sliced and divided

Ice cubes

NOTES

✳ You can use 1 cup (240 ml) of strained roasted lemon juice or 1¼ cups (300 ml) of unstrained lemon juice if you prefer it with pulp.

✳ This recipe can also be used to make traditional lemonade; simply skip the roasting and use fresh lemon juice.

Homemade lemonade just got better. When you roast the lemons, the sugars in the fruit begin to caramelize and add a deep and intense flavor that lends perfectly to lemonade. Another perk of roasting the lemons is that it makes them extremely easy to press for juice, since they're so soft and plump after.

DIRECTIONS

In a pitcher, combine the roasted lemon juice, simple syrup, and cold water.

Slice the lemon into 8 slices and add 4 of the lemon slices to the lemonade, then stir to combine.

Serve in highball glasses with ice and garnish each with remaining lemon slice. Serve with a straw.

SPARKLING BERRY LEMONADE

SERVES 6

INGREDIENTS

4½ cups (1 L) club soda

1 cup (240 ml) Roasted
Lemon Juice (page 167)

¼ cup (60 ml) Raspberry
Simple Syrup (page 160)

¼ cup (60 ml) Blackberry
Simple Syrup (page 160)

¼ cup (60 ml) Strawberry
Simple Syrup (page 160)

2 lemons, sliced and divided

Ice cubes

3 strawberries, halved,
for garnish

This fizzy lemonade recipe is made with three different flavored simple syrups for a juicy beverage that tastes as if it came straight out of the berry patch. The club soda keeps it light and refreshing, while the roasted lemon juice adds warmth and vibrance. An easily crushable and satisfying drink for summer.

~~~~~~~~~~~~~~~~~~~~~~~~~~~~~~~~

DIRECTIONS

In a large pitcher, add the club soda, lemon juice, and all the simple syrups and stir to combine.

Slice each of the lemons into 6 slices. Add the slices of 1 lemon to the pitcher, reserving the rest for garnish.

Pour the lemonade into tall glasses over ice.

Garnish the glasses with the slices from the remaining lemon and a strawberry half.

NOTE
✻ Fresh lemon juice may be used in place of roasted lemon juice, but the flavor will be a bit more tart.

SPARKLING MINT LEMONADE

SERVES 1

INGREDIENTS

Ice cubes

2 oz (60 ml) Roasted
Lemon Juice (page 167)

10 oz (300 ml) chilled club soda

2 oz (60 ml) Mint Simple Syrup
(page 161)

1 mint sprig, for garnish

1 lemon slice, for garnish

Vibrant lemon and cool mint are the perfect pair in this smooth lemonade recipe. Enjoy a single glass on a warm spring day or make a larger batch for showers, Mother's Day brunch, and Derby day.

~~~~~~~~~~~~~~~~~~~~~~

DIRECTIONS

Fill a mason jar or highball glass about halfway with ice.

Pour the lemon juice, club soda, and mint simple syrup into the glass and stir.

Garnish with a mint sprig and lemon slice. Serve with a straw.

LAVENDER LEMONADE

SERVES 6

INGREDIENTS

1 to 1¼ cups (240 ml to 300 ml) Roasted Lemon Juice (page 167, see Notes)

1 cup (240 ml) Lavender Simple Syrup (page 163)

4 cups (960 ml) cold filtered water

1 cup (240 ml) chilled club soda (optional)

1 to 3 drops purple food coloring (optional)

1 lemon, for garnish

Ice cubes

6 lavender sprigs, for garnish

After a trip to our local lavender farm last year, I fell in love with the sweet and warm scent of the fresh blooms. I started making my own lavender syrup for lattes and lemonade, as everyone loves the sweet floral flavor! It's definitely my new go-to for special summer occasions.

DIRECTIONS

In a small pitcher, add the lemon juice, lavender simple syrup, and cold water. If you want a sparkling version, add the club soda. If you want it to be purple, add the food coloring. Stir to combine.

Slice the lemon into 6 slices.

Pour into glasses over ice and garnish each with a lemon slice and sprig of lavender.

NOTES

* You can use 1 cup (240 ml) of strained roasted lemon juice or 1¼ cups (300 ml) of unstrained lemon juice if you prefer it with pulp.

* The pictured drinks have been colored with food coloring for a pretty presentation—this is great for bridal showers. If you're using store-bought syrup, the Torani and Monin brands' lavender syrups are already purple, but the homemade recipe will be clear.

MAPLE LEMONADE

SERVES 6

INGREDIENTS

Ice cubes

4 cups (960 ml)
cold filtered water

1 cup (240 ml) Roasted
Lemon Juice (page 167)

1 cup (240 ml) maple syrup
(see Notes)

2 lemons, sliced and divided

NOTES

* A maple-flavored simple syrup
(Torani brand) or 100% pure
maple syrup can be used in
this recipe.

* If a lighter maple flavor is
desired, substitute the 1 cup
(240 ml) of maple syrup with
½ cup (120 ml) each of maple
syrup and Classic Simple
Syrup (page 158).

There is nothing I'd rather be sipping than a glass of
ice-cold Maple Lemonade. It is both tart and sweet in
the most perfect way, and the flavor is just incredible.
The roasted lemons amplify the coziness of the maple
syrup, and even though maple is technically a flavor
of early spring here in New England, it always reminds
me of fall. But a fresh pitcher of this lemonade is a
welcome sight any time of year!

DIRECTIONS

In a large pitcher, add the ice, water, roasted lemon
juice, and maple syrup and stir to combine.

Slice each of the lemons into 6 slices. Add the
slices of 1 lemon to the pitcher, reserving
the rest for garnish.

Pour into glasses over ice and garnish each with
an additional lemon slice. Serve with straws.

ISLAND PALMER

SERVES 1

INGREDIENTS

Ice cubes

6 oz (180 ml) chilled lemonade

6 oz (180 ml) chilled unsweetened iced tea

1 oz (30 ml) Coconut Simple Syrup (Torani brand)

1 lemon slice, for garnish

This is the kind of drink you'd want to be sipping out of a coconut in a beachside cabana—not too sweet, not too heavy—pure vacation mode. The distinct flavor of coconut rounds out the already popular combination of iced tea and lemonade for a fun and fruity beverage.

DIRECTIONS

Fill a highball glass with ice.

Pour the lemonade, iced tea, and coconut simple syrup into the glass.

Garnish with a lemon slice and serve with a straw. Stir before enjoying.

NOTES

* Storebought lemonade such as Newman's Own can be used in this recipe or you can use the Roasted Lemonade (page 114).

* This drink has a fairly strong coconut flavor, but you can reduce the syrup to just ½ oz (15 ml) for a drink that has just a hint of the tropics.

RASPBERRY ICED TEA

INGREDIENTS

8 cups (2 L) filtered water, divided

8 black tea bags

2 cups (480 ml) Raspberry Simple Syrup (page 160)

¼ cup (60 ml) lemon juice (optional)

Ice cubes

1 lemon, sliced, for garnish

10 to 20 fresh raspberries, for garnish

NOTES

* This tea is best enjoyed within 48 hours.

* The servings for this recipe are easy to adjust; use ¼ cup (60 ml) of simple syrup for every cup (240 ml) of tea.

Of all the berries, raspberries are my favorite. Their balance of sweet and tart makes them a lovely pairing with the bitterness of tea. The black tea base allows the juicy flavor of the raspberry syrup to shine, making this recipe perfect for those who want a fruity, ice-cold glass of something not too sweet on a hot summer day.

DIRECTIONS

In a medium saucepan, bring 2 cups (480 ml) of the water to a boil. Remove from the heat and add the tea bags. Steep the tea for 5 minutes.

Remove the tea bags from the water, being careful not to squeeze them.

Pour the raspberry simple syrup into a large pitcher with the remaining 6 cups (1.4 L) water followed by the tea.

Add the fresh lemon juice to brighten the tea, if desired.

Allow it to come to room temperature before refrigerating for at least 1 hour.

Serve in glasses over ice, garnished with lemon slices and 1 or 2 fresh raspberries.

SPARKLING BLUEBERRY ICED TEA

SERVES 6

INGREDIENTS

4 cups (960 ml) filtered water, divided

4 black tea bags

2 cups (480 ml) club soda

1 cup (240 ml) Blueberry Simple Syrup (page 160)

Ice cubes

24 blueberries, for garnish

6 mint sprigs, for garnish

NOTE

✳ This tea is also delicious with ¼ cup (60 ml) of fresh lemon juice added.

This one is for Maine. The simplicity of this refreshing iced tea is noteworthy because it's lightly sweet with a fresh blueberry flavor that's steady but not powerful. It's the kind of iced tea you want to sit by the water and sip while reminiscing with old friends.

DIRECTIONS

In a medium saucepan, add 2 cups (480 ml) of the water and bring to a boil. Once boiling, remove from the heat and add the tea bags. Steep the tea for 5 minutes.

Remove the tea bags from the water, being careful not to squeeze them.

Add the remaining 2 cups (480 ml) water to a large pitcher, followed by the tea from the saucepan.

Allow the tea to cool to room temperature before chilling in the refrigerator for 1 to 2 hours. Once chilled, add the soda and blueberry simple syrup to the tea and stir to combine.

Pour the mixture into glasses over ice and garnish each with 4 blueberries and a mint spring.

PEACH ICED TEA

SERVES 4

INGREDIENTS

4 cups (960 ml) filtered water, divided

4 black tea bags

½ cup (120 ml) Peach Simple Syrup (page 160)

¼ cup (60 ml) lemon juice

1 lemon

1 peach

Ice cubes

NOTES

✳ Up to an additional ½ cup (120 ml) of peach simple syrup may be added for a stronger peach flavor.

✳ This recipe can easily be doubled for large gatherings.

✳ I have used both Earl Grey and regular black tea to make this recipe and both are delicious.

A classic that celebrates the simplicity of summer and encourages us to slow down, kick our feet up, and savor the sunsets.

~~~~~~~~~~~~~~~~~~~~~~~~~~~~

DIRECTIONS

In a medium saucepan, add 2 cups (480 ml) of the water and bring to a boil. Once boiling, remove from the heat and add the tea bags. Steep the tea for 5 minutes.

Remove the tea bags from the water, being careful not to squeeze them.

Add the peach simple syrup, lemon juice, and remaining 2 cups (480 ml) water into the pitcher followed by the tea from the saucepan.

Allow the tea to cool to room temperature before chilling in the refrigerator for 1 to 2 hours.

Slice the lemon into 8 slices and the peach into 8 wedges. Add 4 of the lemon slices and 4 of the peach wedges to the pitcher and chill for 1 hour before serving.

Pour the tea into tall glasses over ice and garnish each with a lemon slice and peach wedge. Serve with a straw.

STRAWBERRY SWEET TEA

SERVES 8

INGREDIENTS

6 cups (1.4 L) filtered water, divided

8 black tea bags

2½ cups (600 ml) Strawberry Simple Syrup (page 160)

Ice cubes

4 strawberries, halved, for garnish

NOTES

* Store covered in the refrigerator for up to 1 week.

* For a slightly less sweet option you can add 2 additional cups (480 ml) of water and add a ¼ to ½ cup (60 to 120 ml) of lemon juice for some zestiness.

* If you decide to make a Winnie Palmer with this recipe, use 3 cups (720 ml) of black tea and add 3 cups (720 ml) of lemonade.

Southern sweet tea is even sweeter with homemade strawberry syrup, which gives it that extra-juicy punch of sugar. You can also serve it as half tea and half lemonade for a Strawberry Winnie Palmer (see Notes). Either way, it's the perfect batch drink for picnics, BBQs, and beach days!

DIRECTIONS

In a medium saucepan, add 2 cups (480 ml) of the water and bring to a boil. Once boiling, remove from the heat and add the tea bags. Steep the tea for 5 minutes.

Remove the tea bags from the water, being careful not to squeeze them.

Pour the remaining 4 cups (960 ml) of water into a large pitcher, followed by the brewed tea from the saucepan.

Add the strawberry syrup to the pitcher with the tea and stir.

Pour the mixture into glasses over ice and garnish each with a fresh strawberry half.

PARTY PUNCHES

IS IT EVEN A PARTY WITHOUT A BOWL OF PUNCH? I believe that all of life's special occasions are made even sweeter when there's a giant bowl filled with a delicious mix of ingredients to celebrate with. They are easy to make, customize, halve, or double, and a great recipe for eager kiddos to help with! Making punch has always been fun for me—a bottle of this, a bottle of that, and so on until I find a combination of flavors I love and want to share with everyone. And I'm excited to share some of my go-to party punch recipes with you in this chapter—dress them up for the holidays or leave them plain for casual gatherings.

LOVE POTION PUNCH

SERVES 10

INGREDIENTS

6 cups (1.4 L) chilled strawberry soda

2½ cups (600 ml) chilled orange juice

10 scoops vanilla ice cream

1½ cups (360 ml) chilled lemon-lime soda

Sweet clouds of vanilla ice cream float atop a blend of strawberry and lemon-lime sodas and orange juice in this easy Valentine's Day punch, which is a cross between an orange creamsicle and strawberries and cream candy. Kids and adults alike will love the mild and creamy sweetness that gives way to just a hint of tart fruit in this fun party drink.

DIRECTIONS

Pour the strawberry soda and orange juice into a punch bowl that can hold at least 12 cups (2.8 L).

Add the vanilla ice cream to the bowl.

Slowly pour the lemon-lime soda over the top of the ice cream.

Use a ladle to serve in punch glasses. Serve the individual drinks with or without a straw.

LEPRECHAUN PUNCH

SERVES 16

INGREDIENTS

4 cups (960 ml) chilled
white grape juice

2½ cups (600 ml) chilled
limeade (Newman's Own brand)

2½ cups (600 ml) chilled
orange juice

12 drops green food coloring

10 scoops rainbow sherbet

3 cups (720 ml) chilled
lemon-lime soda

2 limes, for garnish

2 clementines, for garnish

NOTE

✳ Lemonade may be used
in place of limeade.

You'll feel like the luck of the Irish is on your side
when you see just how easy it is to whip up this green
sherbet punch for St. Patrick's Day. A sweet blend of
white grape juice, limeade, orange juice, and lemon-
lime soda poured over rainbow sherbet makes for
a frothy holiday drink that will remind people of the
punch recipes popular in the 1950s.

DIRECTIONS

In a large punch bowl, pour in the white grape juice,
limeade, orange juice, and green food coloring and stir
to combine.

Gently drop the scoops of rainbow sherbet on top of
the mixture, then pour the lemon-lime soda over the
top of the sherbet.

Slice each of the limes and clementines into 8 slices.

Use a ladle to serve in punch glasses. Garnish each
drink with a lime and clementine slice and serve with
or without a straw.

EASTER BUNNY PUNCH

SERVES 10

INGREDIENTS

4 cups (960 ml)
chilled orange juice

3 cups (720 ml)
chilled lemon-lime soda

2 cups (480 ml) chilled carrot
juice (Bolthouse Farms brand)

1 cup (240 ml) chilled limeade
(Newman's Own brand)

13 mint sprigs, divided

1 orange

1 lemon

3 limes, divided

Ice cubes

NOTES

* Fresh lemonade can be used
  instead of limeade.

* This can be prepared in a
  large punch bowl with a ladle
  for serving, if desired.

This punch is light, refreshing, and totally springy! It's not overly sweet, but the orange juice and limeade are sweet enough to balance the earthy tone of the carrot juice while still letting the flavor come through. This unique and delicious punch is perfect for Easter and other spring celebrations.

DIRECTIONS

In a large pitcher, add the orange juice, lemon-lime soda, carrot juice, limeade, and 3 of the mint sprigs, then stir to combine.

Slice the orange, lemon, and 1 of the limes, add to the drink mixture, and stir to combine.

Pour into glasses over ice.

Slice the remaining 2 limes into 5 slices each and garnish each glass with a lime slice and mint sprig. Serve with or without a straw.

BRUNCH PUNCH

INGREDIENTS

6 cups (1.4 L) cold coffee
(see Notes)

2 cups (480 ml) half-and-half
or coffee creamer of choice

½ cup (120 ml) Chocolate
Simple Syrup (page 164),
plus more for topping

¼ cup (60 ml) Classic
Simple Syrup (page 158)

1 quart (960 ml) vanilla
ice cream

Coffee Ice Cubes (page 170)

Whipped Cream (page 169),
for topping

NOTE

* You can substitute the
  chocolate and classic
  simple syrups for
  flavored simple syrups
  to change the flavor
  of this punch.

For those not big on fruity punches, this brunch punch
might just be what you're looking for. A unique offering
at any party, guests will love this fun, creamy, and
caffeinated drink. Cold brew coffee is sweetened with
chocolate syrup and simple syrup, with the addition of
half-and-half and finished with vanilla ice cream for an
ultra-velvety finish that's perfect for Sunday brunch,
Christmas morning, and more!

DIRECTIONS

If preparing coffee at home, brew it in advance and chill
for at least 1 hour before using.

In a large punch bowl, whisk together the coffee, half-
and-half or creamer, chocolate syrup, and simple syrup.

Use an ice cream scoop to add the entire quart of ice
cream to the punch, gently dropping the scoops of
ice cream on top of the mixture.

Serve with a ladle into glasses over coffee ice cubes to
prevent dilution. Top glasses with whipped cream and a
drizzle of chocolate syrup and serve with a straw.

SPARKLING SUMMER PUNCH

SERVES 12

INGREDIENTS

Ice Ring (page 171, optional)

4 cups (960 ml) chilled
Roasted Lemonade (page 114)

4 cups (960 ml) chilled
Unsweetened Iced Tea (page 166)

3 cups (720 ml) chilled club soda

1 cup (240 ml) Peach
Simple Syrup (page 160)

Ice cubes

2 lemons, sliced, for garnish

NOTE

* For raspberry iced tea,
use raspberry simple
syrup instead of peach,
or do ½ cup (120 ml) of each
for an extra fruity punch.

When summer is in full swing, this is the punch you
want to be serving at backyard BBQs and block parties.
It's a fun, bubbly twist on the classic iced tea and
lemonade mash-up and you can make it with peach or
raspberry syrup—or both!

DIRECTIONS

If using, prepare the ice ring the day before.

When ready to serve, add the ice ring to a large
punch bowl.

Pour the lemonade, iced tea, club soda, and peach
syrup into the bowl.

Serve with a ladle into glasses over ice and garnish
each glass with a lemon slice. Serve with or without
a straw.

BABY SHOWER PUNCH

SERVES 16

INGREDIENTS

1 packet (.22 oz, 6 g)
blue raspberry lemonade
drink mix (see Notes)

6 cups (1.4 L) chilled
Roasted Lemonade (page 114),
made with regular lemon juice

4 cups (960 ml) chilled pink
or white cranberry juice

10 scoops vanilla ice cream

4 cups (960 ml) chilled
lemon-lime soda

10 mini rubber duckies,
for garnish

NOTES

* I like to use Kool-Aid brand
  blue raspberry lemonade mix;
  however, you can omit it and
  use blue food coloring instead.

* For a pink version, use a
  pink drink mix instead of blue
  raspberry, and a strawberry
  or raspberry lemonade
  instead of regular, or just
  add pink food coloring.

This blue baby shower punch is made with a lemonade
base and "suds" of vanilla ice cream. Partygoers
won't be able to stop talking about how cute this one
is thanks to the mini rubber duckies swimming and
splashing as you ladle this delicious punch into glasses!

DIRECTIONS

In a large punch bowl, add the drink mix, lemonade,
and cranberry juice and stir to combine.

Gently add the scoops of vanilla ice cream on top of
the lemonade mixture so as not to splash.

Slowly pour the lemon-lime soda over the top of the ice
cream to activate the "suds."

Add the mini rubber duckies for decoration and serve
using a ladle. Serve with or without a straw.

TRICK-OR-TREAT PUNCH

SERVES 10

INGREDIENTS

4 cups (960 ml) chilled orange soda

4 cups (960 ml) chilled lemon-lime soda, divided

2 cups (480 ml) chilled pineapple juice

10 scoops rainbow sherbet

Black nonpareils sprinkles, for garnish (optional)

If you find time to throw a party in between all the pumpkin fests, trunk-or-treats, and haunted hayrides, at least it will take you no time at all to whip up this easy punch recipe for all the thirsty zombies, princesses, and dinosaurs in attendance for Halloween.

DIRECTIONS

In a larger punch bowl, pour in the orange soda, 3 cups (720 ml) of the lemon-lime soda, and the pineapple juice and stir to combine.

Add the scoops of sherbet and pour the remaining cup (240 ml) lemon-lime soda over the top of the sherbet.

Top with black sprinkles, if desired.

Serve using a ladle into punch glasses, and serve with or without a straw.

THANKSGIVING PUNCH

SERVES 12

INGREDIENTS

Ice Cups or Ice Ring
(page 171, optional)

3 cinnamon sticks

5 allspice berries

3 whole cloves

3 cups (720 ml) chilled
apple cider

2 cups (480 ml) chilled 100%
unsweetened cranberry juice

2 cups (480 ml) chilled
orange juice

1½ cups (360 ml) chilled
100% pomegranate juice

1½ cups (360 ml) chilled
pineapple juice

2 cups (480 ml) chilled
lemon-lime soda

1 orange, sliced, for garnish

1 cup (100 g) cranberries,
fresh or frozen, for garnish

Ice cubes

With such a bountiful combination of flavors, it seemed fitting to call this one Thanksgiving Punch. However, it's a recipe that encompasses all that autumn has to offer, except pumpkin—that's for pies and lattes. A bit of pineapple juice offers a taste of late summer and orange juice gives way to winter citrus flavors, while apple, cranberry, and pomegranate bridge the gap between the two seasons and highlight all of fall's fruity offerings. Some spices and lemon-lime soda top off this punch with a light yet cozy finish.

DIRECTIONS

If using, prepare the ice cups or ring the day before.

In a large pitcher, add the cinnamon, allspice berries, cloves, apple cider, cranberry juice, orange juice, pomegranate juice, and pineapple juice and chill for 2 hours to let the spices infuse the juices.

Pour the juice mixture into a punch bowl and add the lemon-lime soda, orange slices, cranberries, and ice cups or ice ring, if desired. Stir to combine.

Serve using a ladle into punch glasses over ice.

NOTE

* If you are in a hurry, everything can be poured
straight into a punch bowl and served immediately.

JINGLE BELLS PUNCH

SERVES 16

INGREDIENTS

Ice Cups or Ice Ring
(page 171, optional)

4 cups (960 ml) chilled
pure 100% unsweetened
cranberry juice

4 cups (960 ml) chilled
orange juice

4 cups (960 ml) chilled
lemon-lime soda

2 cups (480 ml) chilled
100% pomegranate juice

2 cups (200 g) cranberries,
fresh or frozen

2 oranges, sliced

16 rosemary sprigs, for garnish

Ice cubes

NOTE

✳ Halve this recipe to make
a pitcher.

This is the punch that started it all. Growing up, my mother's Christmas punch was a holiday tradition in our house—we joke that it isn't Christmas without punch and jelly meatballs. I've tweaked the recipe a bit over the years, and it has now been enjoyed by millions of readers since I published it on my site back in 2016. It includes a simple list of ingredients that pack the festive flavors of cranberries, pomegranates, and oranges into every sip. I make a big bowl each year for our annual Christmas party, and my family never fails to drink every last drop. Serve a small batch from a pitcher or go big with a punch bowl and fancy ice cups or an ice ring!

DIRECTIONS

If using, prepare the ice cups or ice ring the day before.

In a large punch bowl, add the cranberry juice, orange juice, lemon-lime soda, and pomegranate juice and stir to combine.

Add the cranberries, orange slices, and ice cups or ice ring, if desired, to the punch bowl.

Serve immediately using a ladle to add to glasses over ice and garnish with rosemary sprigs. Serve with or without a straw.

MIDNIGHT KISS PUNCH

SERVES 12

INGREDIENTS

12 oz (360 ml) frozen lemonade concentrate, thawed

6 cups (1.4 L) chilled cranberry raspberry juice

6 cups (1.4 L) chilled lemon-lime soda, divided

1 quart (1 L) orange sherbet

1 orange, for garnish (optional)

24 raspberries, for garnish (optional)

NOTES

∗ Serve immediately for best results.

∗ It's best to use 100% juice and not a juice cocktail.

Let's give 'em something to toast about! This party punch is an all-around crowd-pleaser and perfect to serve up while you ring in the New Year. It's like a sweet raspberry lemonade mixed with a creamsicle and a hint of cranberry and lime.

DIRECTIONS

In a large punch bowl, add the lemonade concentrate, cranberry raspberry juice, and 5 cups (1.2 L) of lemon-lime soda and stir to combine.

Top with the entire quart of orange sherbet, using a cookie scoop to distribute.

Pour the remaining cup (240 ml) lemon-lime soda over the top of the sherbet.

Slice the orange into 6 slices, then slice 3 of the slices in half and add on top of the sherbet along with 12 of the raspberries. Slice the remaining 3 slices into quarters and reserve for garnishing the glasses.

Serve using a ladle into punch glasses and garnish each glass with a sliced orange quarter and a fresh raspberry, if desired.

HOMEMADE COMPoNENTS

FOR MANY OF THE RECIPES IN THIS BOOK, you will find that ingredients like soda, juice, simple syrup, and cream are required. Most ingredients will be more convenient and cheaper to purchase at your local supermarket or online. However, some components, such as the Pudding Whipped Cream, you'll need to make yourself, but it is an optional topping and can always be substituted with canned whipped cream for convenience. Many of the other components are also easy and fun to make at home should you choose to. In this chapter, I have compiled a few of my recipes for some of these ingredients if you prefer to make them on your own.

CLASSIC SIMPLE SYRUP

MAKES 1½ CUPS (360 ML)

INGREDIENTS

1 cup (240 ml) water

1 cup (200 g) granulated sugar

DIRECTIONS

In a small saucepan, combine the water and sugar. Cook over medium-high heat for about 10 minutes or until the sugar dissolves and the syrup begins to simmer, stirring frequently so the sugar doesn't stick to the bottom before dissolving. Do not bring to a rolling boil.

Remove the saucepan from the heat and allow the syrup to cool to room temperature, for about 1 hour, before using.

Transfer the syrup over to a bottle or jar and store, sealed, in the refrigerator for up to 3 weeks.

GRENADINE SIMPLE SYRUP

MAKES 1½ CUPS (360 ML)

INGREDIENTS

1 cup (240 ml) 100% pomegranate juice

1 cup (200 g) granulated sugar

1 tablespoon fresh lemon juice

DIRECTIONS

In a medium saucepan, combine the pomegranate juice, sugar, and lemon juice. Cook over medium-high heat for about 10 minutes or until the sugar dissolves and the syrup begins to simmer, stirring occasionally so the sugar doesn't stick to the bottom before dissolving. Do not bring to a rolling boil.

Remove from heat and allow to cool to room temperature, for about 1 hour, before using.

Transfer the syrup over to a bottle or jar and store, sealed, in the refrigerator for up to 2 weeks.

BROWN SUGAR CINNAMON SIMPLE SYRUP

DIRECTIONS

In a small saucepan, combine the water, brown sugar, and cinnamon sticks. Cook over medium-high heat for about 10 minutes or until the sugar has dissolved and the syrup begins to simmer, stirring frequently so the sugar doesn't stick to the bottom before dissolving. Do not bring to a rolling boil.

Remove from the heat and whisk in the vanilla extract for 15 seconds.

Let the syrup cool to room temperature, for about 1 hour.

After cooling, strain through a fine-mesh sieve or cheesecloth-lined funnel into a bottle or jar. Discard the cinnamon sticks.

Store, sealed, in the refrigerator for up to 3 weeks.

MAKES 1½ CUPS (360 ML)

INGREDIENTS

1 cup (240 ml) water

1 cup (200 g) packed dark brown sugar

3 cinnamon sticks

1 teaspoon vanilla extract

FRUIT SIMPLE SYRUP

**MAKES ABOUT 2½ CUPS
(600 ML)**

INGREDIENTS

1 cup (240 ml) water

1 cup (200 g) granulated sugar

2 cups (475 ml) fruit of choice
(see Notes)

DIRECTIONS

In a medium pot, combine the water, granulated sugar, and fruit of your choice. Cook over medium heat for about 10 minutes or until the sugar has dissolved and the fruit is soft and breaking up, stirring frequently so the sugar doesn't stick to the bottom of the pan. Do not bring to a rolling boil.

Remove from the heat and let cool to room temperature, for about 1 hour, in the saucepan.

Strain the mixture through a fine-mesh strainer, squeezing out any excess juice from the fruit.

Transfer the syrup over to a bottle or jar and store, sealed, in the refrigerator for up to 2 weeks.

NOTES

✳ If you are using large fruits, you will want to chop them up into smaller pieces before adding to the saucepan. Pineapple, peaches, and apples can be chopped into 1-inch (2.5-cm) pieces. Strawberries can be quartered and smaller berries, such as raspberries, blueberries, and blackberries, can be left whole. Cherries should be halved and pitted.

✳ This recipe won't work well for making coconut- or lime-flavored simple syrups. I recommend purchasing the Torani brand syrups for those flavors.

✳ Frozen or fresh fruit may be used.

MINT SIMPLE SYRUP

DIRECTIONS

In a small saucepan, combine the water, sugar, and mint. Cook over medium-high heat for about 10 minutes or until the sugar has dissolved and the syrup begins to simmer, stirring frequently so the sugar doesn't stick to the bottom before dissolving. Do not bring to a rolling boil.

Remove the saucepan from the heat and allow the syrup to cool to room temperature, for about 1 hour, in the saucepan.

After cooling, strain the syrup through a fine-mesh sieve or a cheesecloth-lined funnel into a bottle or jar. Discard the mint leaves.

Store, sealed, in the refrigerator for up to 2 weeks.

NOTE

∗ This recipe can be used to make any herb-flavored simple syrup by swapping the mint for an equal amount of another fresh herb. Thyme and basil syrups are other favorites of mine to mix with soda and seltzer!

MAKES 1½ CUPS (360 ML)

INGREDIENTS

1 cup (240 ml) water

1 cup (200 g) granulated sugar

¾ cup (23 g) packed fresh mint

FLAVORED SIMPLE SYRUP

**MAKES 1½ CUPS
(360 ML)**

INGREDIENTS

1 cup (240 ml) water

1 cup (200 g) granulated sugar

1½ teaspoons flavoring extract
of choice

DIRECTIONS

In a small saucepan, combine the water and sugar.
Cook over medium-high heat for about 10 minutes
or until the sugar dissolves and the syrup begins to
simmer, stirring frequently so the sugar doesn't stick
to the bottom before dissolving. Do not bring to a
rolling boil.

Remove the saucepan from the heat and whisk in the
flavoring extract for 15 seconds.

Allow the syrup to cool to room temperature, for about
1 hour, before using.

Transfer the syrup over to a bottle or jar and store,
sealed, in the refrigerator for up to 3 weeks.

NOTE

* This recipe is perfect for making homemade simple
  syrups that are flavored with vanilla, peppermint, or
  almond extract.

LAVENDER SIMPLE SYRUP

DIRECTIONS

In a small saucepan, combine the water, sugar, and dried lavender buds. Cook over medium-high heat for about 10 minutes or until the sugar dissolves and the syrup begins to simmer, stirring frequently so the sugar doesn't stick to the bottom before dissolving. Do not bring to a rolling boil.

Remove from the heat and allow the syrup to cool to room temperature, for about 1 hour, in the saucepan.

After cooling, strain through a fine-mesh sieve or cheesecloth-lined funnel into a bottle or jar. Discard the lavender buds.

Store, sealed, in the refrigerator for up to 2 weeks.

NOTES

* This recipe can also be used for other floral simple syrups; simply swap out the lavender buds for an equal amount of other florals such as rose, hibiscus, or lilac.

* Make sure to use dried petals.

* For larger flowers, use ½ cup (64 g) of petals or crush them so they fill a ¼ cup (32 g) when fairly packed.

MAKES 1½ CUPS (360 ML)

INGREDIENTS

1 cup (240 ml) water

1 cup (200 g) granulated sugar

¼ cup (32 g) dried lavender buds

CHOCOLATE SIMPLE SYRUP

**MAKES 2 CUPS
(480 ML)**

INGREDIENTS

¾ cup (180 ml) water

1½ cups (300 g)
granulated sugar

¾ cup (60 g) Dutch-processed
cocoa powder

1 tablespoon vanilla extract

1 tablespoon light corn syrup

⅛ teaspoon sea salt

DIRECTIONS

In a medium saucepan, combine the water and sugar. Bring to a boil over medium-high heat, stirring frequently so the sugar doesn't stick to the bottom of the pan. Reduce the heat to low and sift in the cocoa powder. Whisk in the vanilla extract, corn syrup, and salt. Continue to cook for about 10 minutes, whisking often, until it starts to thicken.

Remove from the heat and strain through a fine-mesh sieve to remove any clumps. Let it cool completely for 1 to 2 hours before using.

Transfer the syrup over to a bottle or jar and store, sealed, in the refrigerator for up to 2 weeks.

COLD BREW COFFEE

DIRECTIONS

Use a coffee grinder, preferably with a burr grinder over a blade grinder, to grind the coffee beans into coarse grounds, similar to what you would use for brewing hot French press coffee.

Add the coffee grounds and water to either a cold brew coffee pitcher, a 34oz. (1 litre) French press, or a quart-sized mason jar and stir. Cover and steep at room temperature or in the refrigerator for 12 hours.

If using a cold brew pitcher, remove the filter with the coffee grounds. If using a French press, press and pour the coffee into a fresh container. If using a mason jar, line a fine-mesh strainer with cheesecloth and strain into a fresh container.

Store in the refrigerator and use as directed in recipes within 1 week.

MAKES 3 CUPS (720 ML)

INGREDIENTS

¾ cup (66 g) whole coffee beans

3 cups (720 ml) filtered water

UNSWEETENED ICED TEA

MAKES 1 CUP (240 ML)

INGREDIENTS

1 cup (240 ml) filtered water

1 teaspoon loose-leaf black tea, or 1 tea bag

DIRECTIONS

Bring the water to a boil over high heat in a saucepan or teakettle over high heat.

If you are using loose-leaf black tea, add the tea leaves to a tea ball infuser. Add the infuser or tea bag to a mug and pour in the hot water. Allow the tea to steep for 2 to 5 minutes.

Stir the tea and remove the ball or bag; do not squeeze.

Allow the tea to cool to room temperature before transferring to the refrigerator to chill before using.

NOTES

* Multiply as required for each cup needed in the recipe you're making with it.

* Always follow the steeping time recommendations called for on the packaging of your tea of choice.

* Avoid squeezing the tea bag, as it will release a larger amount of tannic acid into the rest of the tea, which can result in a bitter or sometimes sour flavor. Letting the tea sit for too long can also have this result.

* If making a large batch, the tea can be steeped right in the saucepan. Once the tea is done steeping, allow it to come to room temperature in the pan before transferring to a carafe or pitcher and chilling in the refrigerator until ready to use.

* In large batches, the tea can be steeped in a smaller amount of water and then added to additional cold water to cool it down faster.

ROASTED LEMON JUICE

DIRECTIONS

Preheat the oven to 375°F (190°C). Line a 9 x 9-inch (23 x 23-cm) baking dish with parchment paper and set aside.

Wash the lemons, then slice them in half and place them in the baking dish.

Place the baking dish into the oven and roast the lemons for 25 minutes.

Remove from the oven and let the lemons cool for 10 to 15 minutes.

Use a citrus press to squeeze the juice out of the roasted lemons into a liquid measuring cup.

If desired, strain the roasted lemon juice by pouring it through a fine-mesh sieve or use as is if pulp is preferred.

Let cool to room temperature before using in recipes or store in an airtight container in the refrigerator for up to 3 days.

NOTES

* This recipe will yield about 1 cup (240 ml) of strained lemon juice or 1¼ cups (300 ml) of unstrained juice with pulp.

* This recipe can easily be doubled to make a large batch; 10 lemons will fit in a 9 x 13-inch (23 x 33-cm) baking dish.

MAKES 1 TO 1¼ CUPS (240 ML TO 300 ML)

INGREDIENTS

5 small lemons

PUDDING WHIPPED CREAM

**MAKES 2 CUPS
(480 ML)**

INGREDIENTS

1 cup (240 ml) cold heavy cream

1 tablespoon powdered sugar

1 tablespoon instant pudding
powder

DIRECTIONS

In a chilled bowl, beat together the cream, sugar, and
pudding powder for about 2 minutes until thick
and fluffy.

Transfer to a piping bag and pipe onto drinks before
serving.

NOTES

✳ Chill the beaters and a metal bowl in the freezer
for 15 minutes before preparing.

✳ This whipped cream is best used to top milkshakes
and floats.

✳ Store in an airtight container in the refrigerator for
up to 2 days, but note that the texture might thicken
over time.

✳ This recipe is perfect for when you want something
with a little more stability than traditional whipped
cream. Use any flavor of instant pudding you'd like
for your recipe!

WHIPPED CREAM

DIRECTIONS

In a chilled metal bowl, add the heavy cream and vanilla extract and beat on low speed until big bubbles start to form.

Increase the speed to medium, add the powdered sugar, and beat for 2 to 3 minutes until the desired peak structure forms. Scrape down the sides of the bowl as needed.

Add to the top of dirty sodas and milkshakes as desired.

NOTES

* Chill the beaters and a metal bowl in the freezer for 15 minutes before preparing.

* Store in an airtight container in the refrigerator for up to 24 hours—whipped cream may deflate over time.

* You can substitute the vanilla with another flavor extract of your choice. If using another flavor, such as peppermint or almond, only add ¼ teaspoon to start and add more to taste, ¼ teaspoon at a time.

MAKES 2 CUPS (480 ML)

INGREDIENTS

1 cup (240 ml) cold heavy cream

1 teaspoon 100% pure vanilla extract

1 tablespoon powdered sugar

COFFEE ICE CUBES

MAKES 24 ICE CUBES

INGREDIENTS

3 cups (720 ml) coffee

DIRECTIONS

Brew coffee with a coffee machine and allow it to cool to room temperature, or use Cold Brew Coffee (page 165).

Distribute the coffee evenly among the wells of one or two ice cube trays and freeze for at least 4 hours.

Use in coffee drinks as desired.

NOTE

* I recommend removing the ice cubes from the tray once they have frozen, since the oils can stain the tray. They are best stored in an airtight container in the freezer for 2 weeks.

ICE RING & ICE CUPS

DIRECTIONS

To make the ice ring, choose a Bundt pan that fits into your punch bowl.

Layer the bottom of the pan with about four layers of any fruit and/or herbs you may be including and add water until it is just over the fruit.

Freeze until firm, or for 1 to 2 hours, then add more fruit and herbs and fill the rest of the way with water. Freeze until solid, preferably overnight.

To remove from the Bundt pan, quickly dip the pan in a bowl of hot water, then pop out the ice ring into the punch and serve.

If making ice cups, I recommend using smaller pieces of fruit and herbs. Add everything to each cup of a cupcake pan and fill almost to the top with water, then freeze until solid (no layering is required).

NOTES

✳ Using a silicone Bundt pan or cupcake liners allows for easier removal without hot water, since they can just be peeled off of the ice.

✳ You can use this recipe to make a variety of sizes; the amounts of ingredients will vary greatly depending on the pan size you use.

INGREDIENTS

Herbs of choice (optional)

Fruit of choice, sliced as needed (optional)

Water or juice

INDEX

A

allspice: Thanksgiving Punch, 151
apple
  Apple Simple Syrup, 160
  American Pie, 60
  Caramel Apple Lollipop, 44
  Cauldron Bubbles, 56
  Fruit Simple Syrup, 160
  Santa Baby, 63
  Thanksgiving Punch, 151

B

balsamic vinegar: Balsamic Fizz, 81
blackberry
  Blackberry Bramble, 82
  Blackberry Simple Syrup, 160
  Raspberry Lime Rickey, 66
  Sparkling Berry Lemonade, 117
blueberry
  American Pie, 60
  Blueberry Simple Syrup, 160
  Blueberry Lavender Spritzer, 74
  Sparkling Blueberry Iced Tea, 129
butterscotch: Butterbeer, 55

C

caramel
  Butterbeer, 55
  Caramel Apple Lollipop, 44
  Santa Baby, 63
carrot: Easter Bunny Punch, 140
cherry
  Balsamic Fizz, 81
  Black Forest, 59
  Brown Cow Float, 92
  Cherry Simple Syrup, 160
  Dirty Shirley, 27
  Italian Cream Soda, 40
  Malted Chocolate Milkshake, 108
  Raspberry Lime Rickey, 66
  Rocket Pop, 43
  Shirley Temple Float, 96
chocolate
  Birthday Cake Milkshake, 107
  Black Forest, 59
  Brown Cow Float, 92
  Brunch Punch, 143
  Butterbeer, 55
  Chocolate Milk Float, 99
  Chocolate Simple Syrup, 164
  Cookies 'n' Coffee Milkshake, 104
  Malted Chocolate Milkshake, 108

cinnamon
  American Pie, 60
  Breakfast Soda, 31
  Brown Sugar Cinnamon Simple Syrup, 159
  Thanksgiving Punch, 151
club soda
  Blueberry Lavender Spritzer, 74
  Boardwalk Sunset, 52
  Chocolate Milk Float, 99
  Coffee Soda, 69
  Fauxjito, 77
  Italian Cream Soda, 40
  Lavender Lemonade, 121
  Mango Lassi, 28
  Raspberry Lime Rickey, 66
  Sparkling Berry Lemonade, 117
  Sparkling Blueberry Iced Tea, 129
  Sparkling Mint Lemonade, 118
  Sparkling Summer Punch, 144
  Strawberry Colada, 36
coconut
  Bohemian Raspberry, 51
  Coconut Lime Sherbet Float, 100
  Island Breeze, 70
  Island Palmer, 125
  The OG Dirty Soda, 24
  Strawberry Colada, 36
coffee
  Breakfast Soda, 31
  Brunch Punch, 143
  Cookies 'n' Coffee Milkshake, 104
  Coffee Ice Cubes, 170
  Coffee Soda, 69
  Cold Brew Coffee, 165
cola
  Brown Cow Float, 92
  The OG Dirty Soda, 24
cranberry
  Baby Shower Punch, 147
  Jingle Bells Punch, 152
  Midnight Kiss Punch, 155
  Thanksgiving Punch, 151
  Winter Spritzer, 85
cream soda
  Breakfast Soda, 31
  Butterbeer, 55
  Italian Cream Soda, 40

D

Dr Pepper
  Black Forest, 59
  Bohemian Raspberry, 51

The OG Dirty Soda, 24
Southern Delight, 48

G

ginger
  Dirty Mule, 35
  Dirty Shirley, 27
  Shirley Temple Float, 96
grape
  Leprechaun Punch, 139
  PB & J Milkshake, 111
  Purple Cow Float, 103
grenadine
  Dirty Shirley, 27
  Grenadine Simple Syrup, 158
  Rocket Pop, 43
  Shirley Temple Float, 96

L

lavender
  Blueberry Lavender Spritzer, 74
  Lavender Lemonade, 121
  Lavender Simple Syrup, 163
lemon
  Baby Shower Punch, 147
  Balsamic Fizz, 81
  Blackberry Bramble, 82
  Easter Bunny Punch, 140
  Grenadine Simple Syrup, 158
  Island Palmer, 125
  Lavender Lemonade, 121
  Lemonade Float, 91
  Leprechaun Punch, 139
  Maple Lemonade, 122
  Midnight Kiss Punch, 155
  Peach Iced Tea, 130
  Raspberry Iced Tea, 126
  Roasted Lemonade, 114
  Roasted Lemon Juice, 167
  Rocket Pop, 43
  Sparkling Berry Lemonade, 117
  Sparkling Blueberry Iced Tea, 129
  Sparkling Mint Lemonade, 118
  Sparkling Summer Punch, 144
  Strawberry Sweet Tea, 133
lemon-lime soda
  Baby Shower Punch, 147
  Coconut Lime Sherbet Float, 100
  Dirty Shirley, 27
  Easter Bunny Punch, 140
  Jingle Bells Punch, 152
  Lemonade Float, 91
  Leprechaun Punch, 139

Love Potion Punch, 136
Midnight Kiss Punch, 155
Shirley Temple Float, 96
Thanksgiving Punch, 151
Trick-or-Treat Punch, 148
Twilight Swim, 47

lime
Coconut Lime Sherbet Float, 100
Dirty Mule, 35
Easter Bunny Punch, 140
Fauxjito, 77
Island Breeze, 70
Leprechaun Punch, 139
Lime Simple Syrup, 70, 85
The OG Dirty Soda, 24
Raspberry Lime Rickey, 66
Rocket Pop, 43
Shirley Temple Float, 96
Winter Spritzer, 85

M

mango
Mango Berry Splash, 78
Mango Lassi, 28
Mango Simple Syrup, 160
maple
Breakfast Soda, 31
Maple Lemonade, 122
mint
Dirty Mule, 35
Dirty Shirley, 27
Easter Bunny Punch, 140
Fauxjito, 77
Mango Lassi, 28
Mint Simple Syrup, 161
Sparkling Blueberry Iced Tea, 129
Sparkling Mint Lemonade, 118

O

orange
Boardwalk Sunset, 52
Dirty Shirley, 27
Easter Bunny Punch, 140
Jingle Bells Punch, 152
Leprechaun Punch, 139
Love Potion Punch, 136
Midnight Kiss Punch, 155
Orange Dream, 39
Pineapple Orange Float, 95
Thanksgiving Punch, 151
Trick-or-Treat Punch, 148

P

peach
Peach Iced Tea, 130
Peach Simple Syrup, 160
Southern Delight, 48
Sparkling Summer Punch, 144

Twilight Swim, 47
peanut butter: PB & J Milkshake, 111
pineapple
Boardwalk Sunset, 52
Cauldron Bubbles, 56
Coconut Lime Sherbet Float, 100
Fauxjito, 77
Island Breeze, 70
Pineapple Orange Float, 95
Pineapple Simple Syrup, 160
Strawberry Colada, 36
Thanksgiving Punch, 151
Trick-or-Treat Punch, 148
pomegranate
Balsamic Fizz, 81
Grenadine Simple Syrup, 158
Jingle Bells Punch, 152
Mom Juice, 73
Thanksgiving Punch, 151

R

raspberries
Baby Shower Punch, 147
Boardwalk Sunset, 52
Bohemian Raspberry, 51
Fauxjito, 77
Mango Berry Splash, 78
Midnight Kiss Punch, 155
PB & J Milkshake, 111
Raspberry Iced Tea, 126
Raspberry Lime Rickey, 66
Raspberry Simple Syrup, 160
Rocket Pop, 43
Sparkling Berry Lemonade, 117
Sparkling Summer Punch, 144
Twilight Swim, 47
root beer
Brown Cow Float, 92
Root Beer Float, 88

S

shortbread: American Pie, 60
strawberry
Baby Shower Punch, 147
Balsamic Fizz, 81
Boardwalk Sunset, 52
Fauxjito, 77
Love Potion Punch, 136
Mango Berry Splash, 78
PB & J Milkshake, 111
Raspberry Lime Rickey, 66
Rocket Pop, 43
Santa Baby, 63
Sparkling Berry Lemonade, 117
Strawberries & Cream, 32
Strawberry Colada, 36
Strawberry Simple Syrup, 160
Strawberry Sweet Tea, 133

T

tea
Island Palmer, 125
Peach Iced Tea, 130
Raspberry Iced Tea, 126
Sparkling Blueberry Iced Tea, 129
Sparkling Summer Punch, 144
Strawberry Sweet Tea, 133
Unsweetened Iced Tea, 166

V

vanilla
Baby Shower Punch, 147
Birthday Cake Milkshake, 107
Brown Cow Float, 92
Brown Sugar Cinnamon Simple Syrup, 159
Brunch Punch, 143
Butterbeer, 55
Chocolate Milk Float, 99
Chocolate Simple Syrup, 164
Lemonade Float, 91
Love Potion Punch, 136
Mom Juice, 73
Orange Dream, 39
PB & J Milkshake, 111
Pineapple Orange Float, 95
Pudding Whipped Cream, 168
Purple Cow Float, 103
Root Beer Float, 88
Shirley Temple Float, 96
Strawberries & Cream, 32
Twilight Swim, 47
Vanilla Simple Syrup, 162
Whipped Cream, 169

W

whipped cream
Birthday Cake Milkshake, 107
Black Forest, 59
Brown Cow Float, 92
Brunch Punch, 143
Butterbeer, 55
Cookies 'n' Coffee Milkshake, 104
Italian Cream Soda, 40
Malted Chocolate Milkshake, 108
PB & J Milkshake, 111
Pudding Whipped Cream, 168
Whipped Cream, 169

ACKNOWLEDGMENTS

Thank YOU! Thank you so much for choosing this book to add to your home and kitchen. I hope that it will be a fun and trusted resource for you for many years to come. I can't wait to hear all about the recipes that were your favorites and the memories you made with them. I hope that each one brings you joy and good company. Please don't hesitate to reach out on social media or via my website with any questions or to share photos—I love seeing them! See page 176 for my social media handles and website URL.

Thank you to my incredibly awesome husband, Matthew. I could not have dreamed up a better partner for life, business, and parenthood than you—you really are one of a kind. I'm so glad you chose to build this life with me, and grateful to you for indulging all these crazy dreams of mine. I couldn't do it without your constant love and support. Thank you for believing in me harder than anyone else, but also for keeping my wandering artist brain in check—it needs it. I love you and appreciate you more than you know. Cheers to our dreams and whatever comes next.

Thank you to my daughters, Evangeline, Natalie, and Sereia. You are my constant entertainment and motivation. You are all so intelligent, beautiful, and funny. I love watching you grow and discover new things, and I strive to be a better mother and person every day because of each of you. Thanks for constantly reminding me that maybe writing a cookbook with two toddlers and a newborn wasn't my brightest idea. But hey, I did it, we survived, and I love you. Thank you for making life so fun and busy. I wouldn't have it any other way.

And to Shoester, my bestest boy, you've been by my side and underfoot since I started the blog, and I will forever be grateful for your unconditional love and companionship. And Matt, this is published proof that you do rank higher than the dog.

Thank you to the rest of my friends and family, who have been my constant cheerleaders and taste testers—for better or worse—for the last decade. The gratitude I have for each of you is immense, especially my mom and dad—thanks for raising me to be the creative and independent woman I am and always believing in me and my dreams. And to Sam and John, for raising such a good man and always treating me like one of your own since day one.

And to my nana, my biggest cheerleader of all, always, xoxo.

Thank you, Carol, for taking a chance and joining my team. Reconnecting all these years later has been a blessing, and I am so grateful to you for everything you do, but especially for keeping me somewhat organized, even if you don't realize you're doing it. I appreciate your flexibility, patience, and willingness to take on new challenges and learn new things with me. So, if I don't say it enough, THANK YOU!

Thank you, Taylor, for the beautiful author photos and always making me look and feel my best over the last decade! I'm so thrilled you were able to take part in this special project!

Thank you, Camryn and Kaelynn, for wrangling my wild girls all summer. This book was only possible because you two stepped up at the last minute to help entertain them. And for taste-testing ALL of the sodas and giving me the Gen Z stamp of approval!

Thank you to my loyal readers, casual followers, and one-click wonders. I could not do this without you—you are literally the reason I have this amazing career. I am so grateful each day that I have the opportunity to share my love of food and drinks with each of you, and there's nothing better than hearing about how you and yours enjoyed them too.

Thank you to The Quarto Group and Rock Point team; working with you has been a dream come true. I truly could not have imagined a smoother cookbook experience. Thank you to my editorial director, Erin, for discovering and reaching out to me with this idea and for trusting me with the total creative freedom to execute it. To my editor, Keyla, for polishing everything off and being so wonderful and easy to work with; you were so patient and helpful and have my sincerest thanks. And to the wonderful design team, Laura Drew, Tara Long, and Marisa Kwek, thank you for capturing my vibe in the design of this book. It's beyond anything I could have imagined and I love you for it! You guys really are the best publishing team a girl could ask for!

And to God, thank you for Your steadfast love and endless blessings.

ABOUT THE AUTHOR

Rebecca Hubbell started her recipe site, *Sugar and Soul*, in 2013 out of pure boredom while her husband, Matthew, was working long hours as an accountant during tax season. It started as a catchall space and creative outlet, but she eventually found her calling in the food niche, focusing on dessert and drink recipes. Since then, the site has expanded to include savory recipes while still maintaining a passion for all things sweet and bubbly.

A decade later, the site has millions of followers, over fifteen hundred published recipes, and her husband Matthew works on it too—all while raising their three girls, Evangeline, Natalie, and Sereia in Central Maine. It's safe to say, that she's not bored anymore.

To learn more about Rebecca and her recipes visit sugarandsoul.co.

Follow Rebecca on Facebook and Instagram @sugarandsoulco.

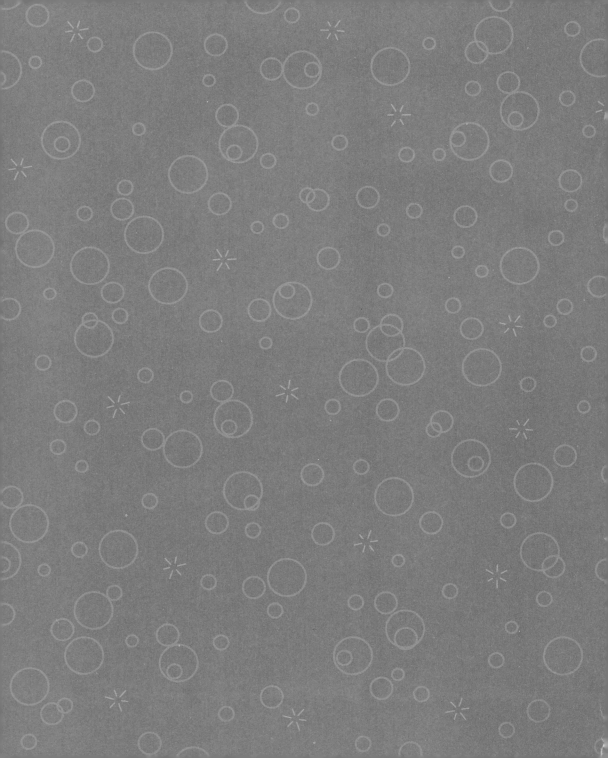